London's 1950s Buses

a class album

Compiled by
James Whiting

Capital Transport

First published 2009

ISBN 978-1-85414-328-0

Published by Capital Transport Publishing
PO Box 250, Harrow Weald, HA3 5ZH

Printed by CS Graphics, Singapore

PHOTOGRAPHS
The following people have been particularly helpful with photo research for this book:

Alan B Cross
Martin Jenkins of the Online Transport Archive
John Laker
Light Rail Transit Association (LRTA)
Seb Marshall
Kevin McCormack

CAPTIONS
The captions have been written by a number of respected writers whose initials appear after the photo credits:

Ken Blacker (KB)
John A Gray (JAG)
Alan Townsin (AT)
Tony Beard (ATB)
Alan B Cross (ABC)
Mike Lloyd (ML)
Laurie Akehurst (LA)

TEXT
Hugh Taylor has been of particular help in tracking down and interviewing some of the authors who have written about their memories of working on the buses in the 1950s. The article by Albert Gunter is an edited version of one that originally appeared in *Illustrated* magazine dated 6th February 1954 and the one by Ted Hearne appeared in the issue dated 3rd July 1954.

Contents

Cover and title page 1950s trips to Uxbridge and Hertford with colour film are two of the features in this book, which has colour photographs of almost every type of London bus running during the decade. *Peter Grace* (cover), *Alan B Cross collection*

Back cover A beautiful shot of RT 4184 on a quiet Sunday in Epping. The origins of the bus stop clearway are in evidence in the broken white line that advises motorists not to park here, though there would be no penalty if they did. *Peter Grace, LRTA.*

In their drab, all-over grey livery, the AEC Regents hired from Leeds City Transport between September 1949 and June 1950 were hardly inspiring to look at. Most carried standard Roe-built bodies which were antiquated looking for their time, but Leeds 201 was the complete opposite and stood out from all the others because of the sweeps and swirls of its exaggerated streamlined appearance. It was a one-off, built by Weymann and exhibited at the 1935 Commercial Motor Exhibition as an example of futuristic thinking; it even had a full width driver's cab until the war. Mechanically and audibly, the Leeds Regents were exactly the same as any standard STL, and they performed adequately on local services from Bromley garage. Leeds 201 was photographed at Well Hall station on 8th January 1950 with Sidcup's year old RTL 31 standing behind.
Clarence Carter/KB

For many years the 35-seater LTs – which were universally known as 'Scooters' – formed the backbone of the Central Bus single deck fleet. Even after the influx of one hundred new Mann Egerton bodied TDs, 98 Scooters remained in service out of the original 201, most of which were extensively rebuilt by Marshall's of Cambridge in 1949. One of the few unrebuilt ones that remained was LT 1428. It had been one of a pair delivered new to London General Country Services in 1932, hence the high fleet number which it did not receive until 1934. LT 1428 survived in service at Sutton garage until the end of 1952 when new RFs came on the scene, and was photographed by the side of Kingston garage carrying its final, unflattering 'all red' livery which it acquired in September 1950. Earlier in that same year all the remaining Scooters had been converted from petrol to diesel using engines taken from scrapped STLs and losing much of their former liveliness in the process.
John Parkin collection/KB

This is a look at a period seen by many as a golden age of London buses. This must partly be because a large proportion of today's bus enthusiasts were born within a few years of the end of the second world war and most of us are able to look back on our childhoods as a time when things were particularly right with the world.

The idea that there was something special about the early post-war years is not entirely without foundation. The pre-war types that were running until the mid-1950s had a lot of character. Some certainly fell some way short of the riding comfort of the RT, RF or Routemaster vehicles, but others have never since been surpassed.

For those to whom the RT family vehicles and the RFs represent the peak of London Transport's bus designs, the 1950s are undoubtedly a golden age. Brand new vehicles of these types were entering service during the first half of the period and by the middle of the fifties they comprised almost all of the bus fleet.

The STD class consisted of three distinctly different looking batches of Leyland Titans, the last of which were the 65 PD1s delivered in 1946. Special design features insisted upon by London Transport, notably the roof route number box, could not disguise the familiar lines of Leyland's standard post-war bodywork, and in fact probably enhanced their appearance. At the time STD 165 was photographed in a still semi-rural corner of Buckhurst Hill, Loughton garage's double-deck fleet consisted entirely of these vehicles, though its drivers were actively agitating for them to be replaced by RTs. With their relatively low power and slow-reacting crash gearboxes, these STDs were satisfactory for quiet suburban operations but not really suited to busy services such as Loughton's 38A which took them all the way through to Victoria. After withdrawal in 1955, all 65 PD1s were sold abroad to end their working lives in Yugoslavia.
Clarence Carter/KB

London Transport's fleet of 4Q4s gave good service and were sound, reliable vehicles although they would win no prizes for good looks. The sloping roof line and untidy window arrangement of their BRCW bodies, coupled with the unusual positioning of the rear wheels right at the back, gave them an ungainly appearance. Q 15 had been withdrawn from country area service towards the end of 1949 but was reinstated to help out at Kingston in March 1950. It remained there for three years, retaining its green livery and gradually getting more dowdy as time went by.
Alan B Cross collection/KB

The downside of this was that by the end of 1955, there was very little variety. We would have to content ourselves with small detail differences between vehicles and the occasional excitement of a new route. The Routemaster promised a little more variety but did not have a big presence in the period under review.

Those who have worked on this book have been fortunate to find a good number of colour photographs from the 1950s, which we present here along with some recollections of the time from people who worked for London Transport as drivers, conductors or men behind the scenes at headquarters offices.

A lot of colour film was not as advanced then as it was to become. Kodachrome shone above all others and we have been lucky to find some early Kodachrome views to include. Other pictures are reproduced from more primitive colour stock, so please make allowance for these in respect of sharpness and colour and for the absence of dates.

Many of the 'sit-up-and-beg' type early STLs lasted well into the nineteen-fifties, their bodies having been heavily reconditioned in the 1947-9 period. Decidedly more old fashioned looking than the well-rounded STLs built from the end of 1934 onwards, their nickname came from the tilted appearance which they gained when converted from petrol to oil in 1939. STL 241, a long term Edgware garage resident and seen at Watford Junction, carried the first version of this body with slightly recessed upper deck front windows, and was one of the last of its class still displaying the black indicator masking introduced in the war which, on most vehicles, had been replaced by red (or green) to match the main body colour from 1946 onwards. STL 241 was not one of those subjected to a major rebuilding, and in its later days it was partly held together by the fitting of heavy metal reinforcement straps to several of the lower deck pillars to help prolong its working life, a short term palliative which was applied to the timber framed bodywork on large numbers of ailing STLs. *Alan B Cross collection/KB*

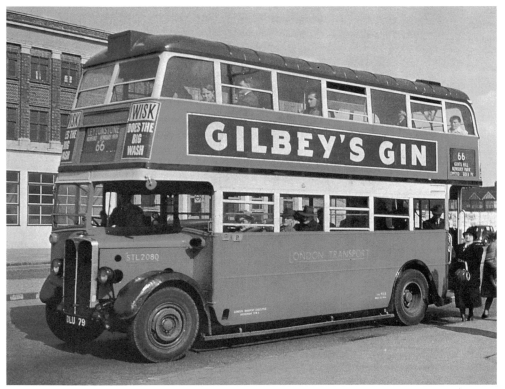

Back in late 1937 London Transport purchased 175 STLs which, though virtually indistinguishable in external appearance from all the others, carried metal framed Park Royal bodies instead of the normal Chiswick built timber framed product. By 1949 these Park Royal bodies had rusted severely and could no longer continue in use, but their chassis were too good to dispose of at a time of acute vehicle shortage. Instead they were given replacement bodies removed from newer STLs which were then being converted into SRTs, resulting in STL 2080 gaining the body from STL 2624 when the latter was converted into SRT 37. Newly repainted in the old red and white livery, it was sent to Forest Gate garage with its 'new' body in March 1949 and is seen on the Eastern Avenue at Gants Hill at work on route 66, which, at the time, was shared with Hornchurch's utility Guys. In this form it was given a short but crucial extension of life, being withdrawn for scrap in November 1950. *Clarence Carter/KB*

Carrying post-war livery and looking fairly healthy, Streatham garage's STL 879 had in June 1948 been heavily reconditioned at Chiswick Works – where it had originally been built thirteen years earlier. STLs such as this, and subsequent variations on the same theme, formed the backbone of the London Transport fleet until mass withdrawals of them commenced in 1950 (a disastrous year for the class in which no fewer than 1,207 STLs were taken out of service). They were comfortable and smooth vehicles to ride in and popular to drive despite the absence of a cab door and the inevitable draughts which this caused. STL 879 is seen at Morden in this typical early nineteen-fifties scene in the company of other STLs, an RT2 and a couple of Daimlers, including one recently demoted from Green Line work at Romford garage. In August 1951 STL 879 received the less attractive 'all red' livery and lasted in service, still on the 118 from Streatham garage, until September 1953. *Alan B Cross collection/KB*

Opposite The twelve 'Godstone' STLs were like nothing else in the London Transport fleet. Both inside and out they looked more provincial than London, and they differed from other contemporary STLs in having crash gearboxes and powerful 8.8 litre engines which made them lively if somewhat mournful sounding performers. Built by Weymann on standard MCW metal body shells, and with the manufacturer's typical ungainly bulging cab line, they were unusual in combining a lowbridge seating layout with a front entrance. No longer required at Godstone on the 410 following the receipt of new RLHs, their careers were briefly revived in September 1950 on the joint services from Addlestone and Guildford garages requiring low height vehicles. In spring 1951, STL 1055 was one of a minority still wearing the old green and white livery, whilst STL 1045 had obtained the later green and cream styling applied when many of the class were overhauled at Reigate in 1949. In July 1951 STL 1055 uniquely gained the unflattering 'all green' livery style, and it was one of four Godstone STLs which were temporarily relicensed during the June 1953 Coronation period, their use in regular service having ceased in October 1952. *Jack Law (Online Transport Archive)/KB*

Above Although not mechanically unlike the 34 'unfrozen' STLs received in 1941/2, the twenty 18STL20s of 1946 bore no outward resemblance to any other double deckers then in the fleet. Their provincial style Weymann bodies made few concessions to London Transport practice and were very distinctive thanks to their flared lower panels. Of all the post-war non-standard classes, these late STLs seemed to fit into the London scene the least well. Hertford garage was a latecomer to their use, in August 1953, which was dictated by a weight restriction on route 327 where a Metropolitan Water Board bridge crossed the New River at Broxbourne. The STLs added a touch of variety to the scene in Hertford bus station compared with the standard RT, RF and GS classes usually found there at this time. They were the last to be withdrawn from passenger service, on 1st June 1955, and all twenty of the class found subsequent use with municipal operators elsewhere in this country. STL 2683 had been fully overhauled in July 1954 when it and its brothers had been expected to remain in the fleet until the end of the decade. *Michael Wickham collection/KB*

The 1950s began with Morden still being served by many pre-war and wartime buses, the latter being the ubiquitous Ds. It was not for nothing that Morden was called 'Daimlerland'. By 1951 all 281 of the D class were allocated to Merton and Sutton garages. D 99 was from the last batch of Brush bodied Ds (D 93-127). Externally there was little to distinguish them from the first batches (D 35-73) except when viewed from the rear. The first batches had angled rear domes and the final batch rounded rear domes. D 99 carries the first livery. This was soon to be replaced by the standard all red livery with cream waist rail as carried by STL 856 standing alongside waiting to depart to Raynes Park on the 157 stand. To the left in the distance is the back of a Sutton STL on route 151 sporting the second post-war livery of upper deck cream windows and cream waist rail. The unsatisfactory loading arrangements at this time and potential danger for intending passengers is illustrated by the narrow strips marked out in white lines. Standing at the Dolly Stop immediately to the rear of D 99 are passengers beginning to queue up for a 93 heading for Epsom. At peak times there would be people milling about all over the place anxious to get home and the reorganisation which was to take place in October 1952 was well overdue. *Alan B Cross collection/ABC*

Morden Station forecourt was a magnet for bus photographers who were able to capture impressive line-ups of different types and liveries. The forecourt lay roughly north to south. North and eastbound vehicles departed from stands facing the north; southbound routes departed from stands facing south. The latter were fine for photographers, especially when the sun was shining. Conversely, trying to produce decent photos of buses on the north facing stands proved difficult and for this reason are much harder to find. In October 1952 there was a reorganisation from which date all stands faced north, a far more practical arrangement from the operating point of view and the safety of passengers, but not welcomed by bus photographers. The original livery adopted for the Green Line Ds was the standard Country Bus livery current in 1946 which was green and off white with black wings and brown roof. The first overhaul cycle took place in 1949. First overhauls emerged in the current Country Bus livery, this time being green and cream with green wings and green roof. However, as the overhaul cycle progressed later overhauls emerged in the current Green Line livery of the day. Examples of both liveries appear in the photo overleaf. *John Parkin collection/ABC*

This group of Daimlers was taken one spring afternoon in 1951. This was a very interesting and colourful period. Thirty-seven Green Line Daimlers had been allocated from new in 1946 to Romford (RE) garage for the 721 group of routes. In December 1948 five Brush bodied Ds were transferred from Merton (AL) to RE and painted in Green Line livery. With the arrival of new Green Line RTs in August 1950 the Romford Ds were steadily withdrawn and stored briefly until December 1950 when they started to arrive at AL. They retained their Green Line liveries, the only changes being to replace the 'Green Line' fleet names on the sides with 'London Transport' fleet names and paint out the Green Line bullseye symbols. For a week or two they would run with no adverts at all, though these were soon to be applied. Now the full complement of 281 Ds was together for the first time, shared between Sutton and Merton garages. A gradual programme to repaint the Green Line Ds into standard red livery ensued over an eight month period, the last becoming red in August 1951. D 133 on the 93 is in the green and cream livery, the D to the far right waiting on the 157 route stand is in standard Green Line green and light green. The Park Royal 'Sutton' D on the left displays the first overhaul livery scheme for this type with cream upper deck windows. D 35 on the 118 is in the final livery to be carried by them. The metal studs set in the roadway in the foreground warn car drivers that there is 'NO PARKING'. The forecourt was LT private property and the Executive was responsible for the maintenance of the whole site, including street lighting.
John Parkin collection/ABC

London Transport lumped all its AEC Regals together in the T class which, with nineteen years separating the oldest from the newest, inevitably spanned a range of body styles. Incredibly 26 of the first batch, built for the LGOC in 1929, lasted in service through to the nineteen-fifties and were even equipped with oil engines from scrapped STLs in May and June 1950. This impeded their previously lively performance somewhat, but gave them an extended lease of life by the end of which they were amongst the most antiquated looking single deckers still running anywhere in the British Isles. Seen terminating in Kingston is the pioneer of the class, T 1, and the absence of an Autovac tank from the front bulkhead confirms that it is now oil engined. Despite having been renovated by Kenex Ltd at Ashford in 1948, its roof has developed a heavy sag confirming the toll that almost two decades of active service has taken on its Chiswick-built body. *Alan B Cross collection/KB*

As a means of seeing them into the nineteen-fifties, eighteen of the original T type were sent to Marshall's at Cambridge in 1949 for their bodies to be extensively reconditioned. Specified as being to 'new build' standard, these were in fact almost new bodies with little remaining of the old apart from the retention of their original distinctive shape. Flush side panelling and new-style livery made them instantly recognisable from outside, but the main alteration was internal where they were totally updated in current RT styling, even to small items of detail such as polished bracelets separating the change of colour mid-way up the window pillars. Only the original seats were retained, but now covered in RT-type moquette. The early Ts were retained at Kingston garage for operation on routes 218 and 264 across Walton-on-Thames bridge on which a weight restriction applied, but on this occasion T 28 is about to perform a run on the 215 to Church Cobham. It lasted in service until January 1953 by which time a new, temporary bridge had been put in place at Walton. *Alan B Cross collection/KB*

Due to its deteriorating condition, unrebuilt T 31 was withdrawn from passenger service in October 1951 but it continued to be active right up to May 1956 as an occasional driver trainer and general runabout. It was even repainted during this time in its own unique livery of all-red with black relief band and brown roof. Still in the fleet three years after all the other early Ts had been sold, it became an object of some curiosity and was duly bought by Ken Blacker and a small consortium of friends with the idea of preserving it for the future. This was the event which really marked the start of private bus preservation, though the group had no inkling at the time of the huge preservation movement that would eventually develop from it. When they drove T 31 away from Norbiton garage in October 1956 for temporary storage at Swiss Cottage, they had no idea of the dire state of its bodywork. This only came to light when, upon removing the outside panels, huge chunks of rotted pillar came away too. The problems of preserving old, wooden framed buses were learnt the hard way. *LRTA/KB*

Top left The famous 10T10 class, of which 266 were built in 1938, represented the archetypal Green Line coach, and they dominated the majority of Green Line workings until the RFs came along in 1951/2. They were handsome, comfortable, functional, and ideal in every way for the purpose they were meant to serve. Powered by 8.8 litre oil engines, they were well adapted to the quite commanding Green Line schedules, though they were not perhaps quite as fast as the superb underfloor engined Leyland TFs. Their subsequent demotion to bus working was accompanied, in some cases, by an unfortunate downgrading including removal of their heaters and replacement of their linoleum floor coverings by plain wooden slats. Still in two-tone Green Line colours, T 610 awaits departure at Guildford on the attractive 425 run to Dorking with one of Aldershot & District's typical Dennis Lancets in the background. Officially demoted to bus status in May 1952, T 610 was a long term Guildford garage resident and often worked on Green Line route 715 which was otherwise the sole preserve of Q-types. The reason for this was that a single 715 duty was linked for schedule purposes to a journey on the 425 on which the Qs were not type approved. *W.J.Wyse/KB*

Left The fifty AEC Regals allocated by the Ministry of War Transport to the LPTB for 1946 delivery were classified as 14T12, and though really only intended as a stop-gap measure pending the post-war fleet renewal programme, they served a useful function for more than a decade. They carried Weymann's own standard design of metal framed body, adjusted slightly to suit London Transport's destination indicator requirement which resulted in an unfortunate frowning appearance at the front and gave an awkward upward sweep on the indicator box at the rear. These were the first motor buses in the fleet to be delivered with provincial-style sliding windows instead of half-drops, and by using copious amounts of varnished woodwork in the interior Weymann further enhanced their 'provincial' feel. Their combination of 7.7 litre engine and crash gearbox meant that their road performance was nothing spectacular, but they proved to be sturdily-built and reliable vehicles. Whilst working from Uxbridge garage, its last allocation in London service, T 749 shares a stop at the old Hounslow West terminus of the Piccadilly and District lines with RT 2284 in 1958. *Marcus Eavis (Online Transport Archive)/KB*

Above London's last Ts, the thirty 15T13s purchased for country service in 1948, were the liveliest and smoothest of all. Based on the Regal Mk III chassis and fitted with 9.6 litre engines and preselector gearboxes, they were in every way comparable to the RT specification but had the weight advantage of only having to carry a 31-seat body. In early post-war years London Transport had a close working relationship with Mann Egerton of Norwich who heavily reconditioned several hundred double deckers, and they also built the timber framed bodies on the 15T13s to their own workmanlike design but incorporating many LT features, especially concerning the interior fixtures and decor. Originally in a green and white livery, they later received the standard 'all green' style, and in later years their appearance was enhanced by the fitment of rear wheel trims. T 779 is seen at Hemel Hempstead on what – judging by its running number HH 202 – is a relief working to Watford. A long term resident at Hemel Hempstead, it spent its last few months at Kingston in 1957/8 – still in green livery – before being sold, like T 749 on the opposite page, for further service in Ceylon (now Sri Lanka). *Geoff Morant/KB*

A Trip to the States in Three London Buses

Ted Hearne

Driving into Cricklewood garage on Boxing Day 1951, I was told that the Divisional Superintendent wanted to see me next day. I smelled trouble, but I comforted myself with the knowledge of a twenty-nine years' clean driving record and the fact that I had recently been given the Bronze Cross for twenty-five years' safe driving.

Next day the superintendent looked up from his desk and asked me as I came in: "Like to go to the United States, Hearne?" At first I thought he was joking. Then I learned I was one of a small London Transport team picked to drive three double-deckers on a ten thousand mile goodwill mission from New York right across the United States. I was amazed, and told him so.

We arrived at New York on the night of 17th March 1952, but everyone agreed that it would be wrong to unship red buses on St Patrick's day! So we went to the New York Licensing Department where we had to fill in a questionnaire asking what we'd do in certain driving conditions, and were each given an eyesight and colour-vision test.

Then each of us was taken outside by a uniformed examiner and told to drive off in a left-hand drive Austin. "You're a good driver," I was told, "but why so cautious?". I had to explain that London buses weren't fitted with bumpers and that, in any case, private cars did not use their bumpers to jockey other cars for position on the roads of Britain. It was a long time before the examiner really believed me. The following day, before we could drive the buses away from the docks we had to deal with scores of newspaper reporters, cinema people and broadcasters, all of whom asked dozens of questions about the buses.

One of the three, the 'crew-bus' we called it, had had the top deck altered so that each of us had a space for our clothes and kit while we were on the tour. The lower deck had been converted into a workshop. The top deck of the second bus was laid out as a travelling exhibition with pictures of places of historic interest or beauty in Britain; and, downstairs, as an office from which visitors could get information about travel facilities in Britain. The third bus was kitted out as a good old No. 11 – complete with blinds showing its destinations, advertisements, and even stocks of tickets which we punched out as souvenirs.

After giving the buses a final polish we drove out into the New York streets. We had a convoy of mounted police, police in cars, and police on motor cycles. Thousands of New Yorkers, astonished at the sight of the big, red double-deckers – for they had seen few double-deckers at all and no 'London reds' – were cheering on each side. The whole thing was like a small Lord Mayor's procession.

Our first stop was the Fifth Avenue Coach Company's garage near Central Park – one of the few garages in all America high enough for a London bus to enter. After that each driver was given a separate itinerary. My job was to drive out to a polio hospital on the outskirts of the city.

The first thing I noticed was that there was no jay-walking in New York. For a London bus driver it was wonderful not to have people dodging across in front of the wheels all the time. I was also impressed by the traffic lights. Many had no amber and just changed direct from red to green and back again – which meant that you had to look nippy.

We got to the hospital without trouble and parked in the big quadrangle there so that the kids who were not confined to their beds could look at the big, bright-red bus. They

marvelled at it, as they had never seen anything like it in their lives. Some of the children couldn't get to the windows, so we gave them little clockwork model buses.

On my way back from the hospital I had an example of what we were to meet often in the tour that followed. We were entering the city when, just ahead, I spotted an elevated railway crossing the road by a low bridge. "We won't get under that," I told the New York bus chief who was with me. I was right – U.S. laws demand only twelve feet six inches clearance, whereas a London bus needs fourteen feet six inches – so I had to reverse three hundred yards up a one-way street.

This question of clearance was one of our main problems in America. In fact, the eight thousand mile tour of the United States – so successful that a two thousand mile tour of Canada was added, finally came to twelve thousand miles and many of the additional two thousand miles can be blamed on detours necessitated by the height of the bus. Wires, cables and bridges all forced us to take alternative routes.

What's more, in the Sierra Nevadas we took the buses up to more than seven thousand feet. We went up to over eight thousand crossing the Rockies on our way back to New York, and we got through one long rock-tunnel near Lake Tahoe, Nevada, with only an inch or so to spare between the bus top and the roof of the tunnel.

We began and finished in New York and one thing says a lot for the London buses. We never had to undo the spare parts kit, and we didn't even have a puncture during the whole twelve thousand miles.

Following their trip to North America, RTs 2775 and 2776 and RTL 1307 are seen parked at Earl's Court. RT 2775 provided facilities for the crew on the upper deck and a maintenance workshop on the lower deck, which has blacked out windows. Blacked out windows are also on the top deck of RTL 1307 which was fitted out with an exhibition promoting tourism to Britain.

A Day at Hertford, June 1951

Alan B Cross

A front-entrance STL, a 6Q6, an RT and two 10T10s in Hertford bus station, June 1951. Nine months later, TFs working as buses would start to appear as well, as they were released from Green Line work by the arrival of the new RFs.
Alan B Cross collection/ABC

In June 1951, when the photographs in this feature were taken, there was still plenty of variety for the enthusiast visiting Hertford bus station in contrast to the high level of standardisation by the middle of the decade. Apart from some new RTs, it was still served by pre-war vehicles of many types, including 9T9s, 10T10s, Qs and my beloved Cubs. Some red STLs were in evidence at this time and a few TFs had arrived; more would be released from Green Line service by the new RFs later that year. Some of these TFs kept their Green Line livery; others were repainted in all-over country bus green with a thin cream band on the beading below the windows. By the end of 1953, all of the pre-war vehicles had disappeared.

The bus station was fine for bus spotters, but not so good for photographers when the sun was shining because of the direction in which the bus stands faced. Wartime metal bus shelters obscured the nearside of the buses, leaving little option other than to take offside photos. For much of the day this meant shooting into the sun, with unhappy results. A saving grace was that incoming buses had an unloading stand at an angle to the main stands, allowing nearside shots with better lighting.

The photographic trip to Hertford with colour film happened before the transfer of TFs to bus work at various garages, including HG where they arrived the following March. If one felt like a prince when riding in a 10T10, then one felt like a king travelling in a TF. There was a solitary double seat immediately to the left of the entrance. This was the place to bask in the smooth ride, almost like floating along in a marshmallow, and the quiet engine. The visibility through the nearside front window was superb, there being no bonnet to obscure the view ahead.

The unusual design of the entrance on STLs like STL 1510 was intended to prevent draughts within the lower saloon but it was quickly realised this had not been achieved. A warm breeze flowing in during the summer was welcome, but sitting downstairs in the winter was another matter and to be avoided if at all possible. Forward visibility from the nearside seats was poor because of the inward facing bulkheads either side of the entrance step. The nearside front main bulkhead was divided and part angled inwards towards the entrance step, resulting in a further pillar obscuring the view. Forward viewing from the first offside seat was almost impossible because the staircase to the upper deck was immediately in front and blocked the view. These STLs were all built with a luggage space under the staircase and additional luggage shelves over the rear wheel arches. The first batch of bodies built by Chiswick had these removed in 1939 and replaced by inward facing seats over the wheel arches, increasing the total seating from a meagre 48 to 52. The second batch of bodies, this time by Weymann, retained the luggage shelves throughout their lives and remained 48 seaters. Immediately behind the entrance there was a single seat, opposite which was the foot of the stairs to the upper deck. Climbing the stairs took passengers through a 180 degree turn, arriving at the top facing two single seats. Turning to the right past these brought one to the pair of front seats, both ideal for bus spotting on the journey. Another unusual feature of these STLs was the bench seat across the rear of the upper deck, officially seating five but often a bit of a tight fit if some of the five passengers were a little on the portly side.
Alan B Cross collection/ABC

Above At one time or another Hertford garage operated most types of standard rear-entrance STLs. Exceptions were Tunnel, Tilling, 'General', unfrozen and low-bridge models. Starting with deliveries in 1934 (STL 609 onwards) visibility from the lower saloon front nearside seat was good due to the front bulkhead window sloping downwards to the nearside from the central pillar. The same was true for the offside where one could get a good view of the driver and his handling of the vehicle. Hertford had some of the earlier 'sloping back' bodied STLs (STL 427 on loan from the central area is shown above) and an inward groan was given on seeing one of these approaching. These had higher waistrails and even higher front bulkheads than later models. High waist rails combined with the low wooden framed seats meant that passengers sat so low that even adults of short stature could just about see through the lower deck windows. Even worse, the front bulkhead windows were higher still. Upstairs was fine, the waistrails being the same depth as later types. *Alan B Cross collection/ABC*

Above right and right Front downstairs nearside seats on later STL bodies such as those carried by STLs 1859 and 1807 were often sought after not only for observation but, especially in winter, for the warmth rising from the flywheel cover which protruded from the front bulkhead into the saloon. It was offset slightly to the nearside, so much so that passengers sitting on the gangway side of the nearside seat could not put their right foot on the floor and had no choice other than to place it on the flywheel cover. Then there was the pleasure of being the closest one could be to the singing sounds and warm smells from the engine and gearbox and to watch the driver selecting the next gear in advance with the gear lever and not depressing the operating pedal at the same time. This was a source of mystery to me for some time, not understanding the operation of a 'pre-selector' gearbox. The upstairs seating was unusual. The rearmost seat was a normal double, situated over the staircase well. In front were two single seats which one had to pass between to reach the rearmost seat. These single seats were comfortable and one could spread out. However, the single seat adjacent to the staircase well faced right down the central aisle and one could feel slightly isolated. Alighting passengers looked straight at you as they came down the aisle to go downstairs. For anyone who collected tickets the rearmost seat was worth exploring when no one was looking. This seat did not have legs but was built on a box. If the STL was one with metal framed seats, the seat squab could be lifted out easily and sometimes in the darker corners of the space below could be found tickets several years old, albeit sometimes a little grubby. *Alan B Cross collection/ABC*

Left To describe the 9T9 model as the poor man's 10T10 is a bit unkind. Originally built for Green Line work, these vehicles had the deeper and more comfortable seats which were retained after demotion to bus work. It was comforting to settle into the deep seat squabs and look around. Very prominent was the huge circular grille of the Clayton Dewandre heater, set into the front bulkhead above the flywheel housing. The original pre-war green linoleum flooring had been replaced after the war with wooden slatted flooring and all the ashtrays removed from the seat backs. One could see where they had been as they had left indentations in the moquette on the seat backs. This moquette had faded slightly over the years and the original colours could be seen where the ashtrays had been fitted. This moquette added to the feeling of comfort and placed the 9T9 apart from normal service buses which only had rexine on the seat backs. Most single deck types carried the fare board on a central panel on the front bulkhead. In the case of the 9T9 this position was already occupied by the heater, so it was positioned on the rear emergency exit door. When riding on single deckers at the front, one of the pleasures was studying the fare table for the route, something denied when riding on 9T9s. On moving off one was at once aware that the pulling power of the engine was a little sluggish and less smooth compared with the 10T10. In post war years some of the class lost their front bumpers, which did not improve their frontal appearance. Perhaps the best view passengers had was on the first of the four pairs of seats which were raised up over the wheel arches at the rear. Here one could look over all the passengers seated in front at the lower level and feel slightly superior. *Alan B Cross collection/ABC*

Below It is unlikely the average passenger arriving at Hertford Bus Station on a 9T9 to do some shopping and returning home on a 10T10 would have noticed any difference between them. But not so the enthusiast. If he had the choice of riding on a 9T9 or a 10T10 it is very likely there would be little hesitation on which to choose. Mechanically more powerful, the 10T10 engine had a sweetness of tone second to none. The outward body design was most pleasing. One felt the 9T9 did not quite make it in appearance compared with the 10T10. All in all the 10T10 won hands down. The two types were very similar internally. Most noticeable would be the absence of the Clayton Dewandre saloon heater on the bulkhead, replaced by the fare board, now in the conventional location. Flooring was still of green linoleum which added to the feeling of elegance. *Alan B Cross collection/ABC*

Above Hertford and Guildford garages shared the operation of the 715 Green Line route between the two towns using 6Q6s. These were also used on local Hertford routes and it would have been possible to see a Green Line Q side by side with an earlier Country Bus Q in Hertford Bus Station, both running on route 372 to Welwyn Garden City. When riding in a 6Q6, one's first reactions were of a noisy, airless ride in an interior lacking personality. Facing you as you climbed up the two entrance steps was a longitudinal seat for four. The seat was provided with arm rests like Underground carriage seating. This set of seats was situated over the engine and one was very conscious of the noise underneath, and the warmth generated. On the nearside between the entrance and cab bulkhead was a longitudinal seat for two. If one could get to this seat there was a good view of the driver but looking out at the road ahead meant turning one's head to the left and after a while the result was a crick in the neck. The remainder of the saloon had conventional pairs of seats facing forward but, unlike the 9T9s and 10T10s there was no raised section over the rear wheels. The driver entered the cab through a door in the centre of the bulkhead. Apart from that the front cab was not unlike a trolleybus, and possibly large items of luggage were carried in the empty area in the nearside of the cab which could not be fitted onto the luggage racks above the seats. In post-war days these Qs had RT style moquette, very ordinary compared with the pre-war 9T9s and 10T10s which had a muted striped pattern with more subtle warm tones. *Alan B Cross collection/ABC*

Upper right and right The Cubs were cosy intimate vehicles which ambled around narrow country lanes serving villages which would otherwise be cut off from their local town – in this case Hertford. These were genuine 'pay as you enter' buses. It was quite common to see a C and a T parked side by side in Hertford Bus Station. It was then that one realised how diminutive the Cubs were. This was very noticeable from the rear, the 10T10 appearing to tower over the Cub. A case of 'Little and Large'. Despite the ceiling being so much lower in a Cub there was still a feeling of spaciousness though it did seem a little cramped when there was a full complement of 20 seated passengers and several standees. Looking in through the entrance one faced the driver's seat. This was hinged to allow access to the batteries which were housed in the box which formed the base of the seat. On the panel below the driver's offside sliding window was a hook from which the running card could be hung. On the moulding above his side window in white letters and figures were (to the left) the allocated garage code and (to the right) the bus body number. In service the passenger climbed the single step and offered his fare to the driver. His ticket rack was on a ledge on the dash in front of the steering wheel and his money bag over his shoulder. On the dash was the solitary instrument – the ammeter. The fare table was on the left side of the entrance. Behind it and out of sight was a wooden rack where the driver could put his ticket rack when leaving the bus unattended. No speedometer was fitted and may not have been considered necessary. It is doubtful whether speeds much in excess of 30 mph were generally reached in service. On the left-hand side of the small driver's bulkhead hung a folded brown curtain. This was hung from domestic type curtain runners on a brass rail and was drawn across to the left of the driver at night time to screen out reflections from the interior lights. The Cub gave a comfortable ride. With luck one could bag the single seat immediately behind the entrance from whence the view ahead, the driver double-declutching on each gear change and the throaty roar of the Leyland diesel engine all gave immense pleasure. Like many rural routes, the driver knew his regulars and an atmosphere of friendliness spread throughout the bus. An everlasting memory is the sound of the Hertford Cubs revving up at the unloading stand and the roar of the Leyland engine as the driver raced across the car park in second gear to reach the route 333 stand on the other side. *Alan B Cross collection/ABC*

Around the time the order was placed for the RFs, the Ministry of Transport agreed that the maximum length of a single decker could be increased from 27ft 6ins to 30ft, but it was decided not to risk delaying the sightseeing batch of 25 vehicles to benefit from this change because these were needed for the Festival of Britain in summer 1951 along with the RFWs. Both types arrived just in time. Colin Curtis, who was later to become the owner of RF 19 as a preserved vehicle and was one of a two-man team from Chiswick to collect RF 1 from Metro-Cammell, remembers being struck by the grey and green livery, thinking that it did not look like a London Transport vehicle. He remembers being impressed by the ride back to Chiswick, particularly the deep cushion seats. RF 19 is seen on a private hire soon after delivery. All 25 of these RFs were to be allocated to Central Bus garages and were intended for use on excursions, tours and private hire duties, which merited their predominantly green livery. A slight nod to the central area was made in the red lining and red fleet names. These 25 coaches were the first vehicles in the London Transport fleet other than trolleybuses to have registration numbers containing the digits of the fleet numbers. The next batch of RFs did not follow suit but the matching numbers returned later in the RF production batch. *Jack Law (Online Transport Archive)/JW*

About eight years later, RF 19 picks up passengers at Cowley while running on route 458 from Uxbridge to Slough. This was one of ten of the 35-seater private hire coaches modified for Green Line work in May 1956. In early 1959 all remaining crew operated Country Bus RFs were adapted for one-man operation. Consequently RF coaches that had been displaced from Green Line relief duties by RTs worked the remaining crew operated routes 391/A, 447 and 458. The provision of the brackets for fixing the Green Line side route boards can clearly be seen and the design differed from those on the standard Green Line RF. *Peter Grace/LA*

Upper left Clapham Common sees Green Line RF 56 heading from High Wycombe to Reigate on route 711 passing RTL 1019 on tram replacement route 155 heading for Victoria Embankment via Westminster Bridge. The RF is in its original condition with the style of black and amber blinds introduced in May 1946 and the green side route boards. The coach has not yet been fitted with a black horizontal rail to the nearside windscreen, a safety modification applied at an early stage following an accident involving a conductor. *W.J. Wyse/LA*

Left In September 1956 ten RF country buses were transferred to Sidcup central area garage in order to release red RFs for overhaul. RF 564 stops in Station Road, Sidcup with one of its red cousins behind while working on route 241, which ran from Welling Station to Sidcup Garage. The route was required to be worked by single deckers due to a low bridge at Sidcup Station. In order to comply with Metropolitan Police requirements the platform doors of the green RFs were kept permanently open while working on central area routes. The bus returned to the country area in February 1958. *Alan B Cross collection/LA*

Above The pleasing appearance of the RF class is demonstrated in this view of an immaculate RF 353 turning from Clarence Street into London Road, Kingston. The bus was allocated to Sutton after its overhaul in May 1957 and is seen working on route 213 during that summer. Note that at this location there are no trolleybus traction poles as the span wires are attached to the building. This arrangement was something of an exception to the rule but was used in various locations, usually where the pavement was considered too narrow or, in this case, where the shop canopy formed an obstruction. *LRTA/LA*

Opinions vary about the external appearance of the RFW 39-seaters and whether, as successors in London Transport's small luxury hire coach fleet to the LTC six-wheelers, they came up to the same high design standards. Certainly they looked like nothing else ever dreamt up by London Transport or manufactured by Eastern Coach Works. However they were undoubtedly very comfortable, especially if a fairly long journey was to be undertaken, and they were reasonably speedy although their 8 tons 5 cwt unladen weight and extra 6 inch width compared to the standard RF made them seem a little ponderous. However for pottering around on a guided tour of London Airport, such as RFW 8 was doing in the days before high security banned such jaunts, a great degree of luxury was hardly needed. RFW 8 was new in 1951 and was allocated to several central bus garages during that decade although, in the absence of garage plate holders, there is no external clue as to which garage it belonged. The semaphore-type trafficator indicators, which were never much favoured by London Transport, were often troublesome or accident prone, and the offside one on RFW 8 has not returned fully into its slot. *Geoff Morant/KB*

Sixty-five of these 'one-and-half-deck' vehicles were operated by London Transport for their owners, British European Airways. Coded 4RF4, there was much LT influence in their design and the result was rather more elegant than most vehicles of similar layout. They were bodied by Park Royal on similar chassis to the RFWs (which were 3RF3s). These airport buses seated 16 passengers in the front half of the lower deck and 21 upstairs above a luggage compartment which occupied the rear half of the lower deck. Housed initially at Gillingham Street (Victoria) garage, they connected central London with London (Heathrow) Airport and this view is at the Waterloo Air Terminal. The vehicles moved from Victoria to Shepherd's Bush garage in October 1957 in connection with the move of the London starting point of the service to Cromwell Curve near Earl's Court and to Hammersmith in July 1960 when the former trolleybus depot there became available. *Bruce Jenkins/JW*

The Man who Jumped Tower Bridge with an RT

Albert Gunter

When I saw the road sinking away in front of me I thought I was dreaming. Then I realised that the northern arm of Tower Bridge, the arm on which I was driving, was steadily rising. My front wheels were only a few feet from the edge of the arm. I had crossed that bridge thousands of times – not only in my six years as a bus driver, but also in twenty years' driving before that, including a wartime spell in the London Fire Service. Normally, warning lights at each entrance to the bridge turn orange, then red. A loud warning bell rings, then an official ties ropes across each entrance to the bridge.

This time, on a dry December day in 1952, taking a 78 bus on the last run from Shoreditch to Dulwich, I found the lights green. There was no warning bell, no rope. My speed was about twelve miles an hour when the bridge started to lift. Instinctively, I knew the best thing was to accelerate so I put my foot down.

As I speeded up, the steadily rising arm from which we took off was only about three feet above the rest of the bridge. Thank heavens I didn't try to brake! We would still have gone over the edge – but would have been quite a bit higher when it happened.

All the same the drop was quite enough for a seven-and-a-half-ton vehicle. Inside the bus, my conductor thought we were in for a wet finish in the Thames. The few passengers were being thrown around like sacks of feathers.

We crash-landed with a tremendous clatter, but the vehicle kept upright. I parked at the side of the road beyond the bridge. As I climbed down, a policeman ran up shouting, "Driver, stop the traffic!" I saw to it that nothing came on to the bridge from our side.

Within a few minutes the fire brigade, ambulances and more police arrived. My conductor had a broken heel bone – he was the only person on the bus who was standing at the time of the jump – and one boy had a fractured arm. Otherwise, the few passengers suffered only minor injuries, although all of us were taken to hospital and treated for shock. A few hours later I was home.

Strangely enough, not a pane of glass in the bus was broken. Some of the seat cushions had been thrown forward, but everything else looked normal. It was only after a fitter had come out and taken the vehicle carefully back to Dalston garage that we knew the extent of the damage. The chassis had been split in two and all the springs had broken.

There were one or two interesting sequels. I told my story on the radio in *Woman's Hour*, and later a Londoner who owns a hotel at Bournemouth offered my wife, two children and myself a free week's holiday, and treated us magnificently. London Transport gave me £10 – I was off work for ten days as a result of the incident – and the City Corporation gave me £35. I found that there was one special reason why everyone was so glad that the accident had passed off so well. For the first time in living memory there had not been a fatal accident on the roads in the City of London during that year – and it was December 30th when we jumped the bridge. It would have been just too bad if this fine record of safety had been broken so near to the year's end.

Right Not the bus that jumped Tower Bridge, but RT 2653 crossing the bridge on the original London sightseeing tour, which began life in 1951 as a numbered excursion. *Peter Grace/JW*

The majority of RT-family bodies were built by Park Royal or Weymann, but only the latter produced examples in country area green livery. The first country RTs were of RT3 type with roof-mounted route number boxes, but from RT 1012 onwards the revised RT3/1 body, as shown here, was introduced; this had the familiar layout that was to remain standard for the remainder of the production. Early deliveries still featured wartime restricted blind displays and Epping garage's RT 1023 demonstrates this. Epping received its first RTs, RT 1015–1025, in November 1948 and this picture illustrates an example in original condition with the small headlamps (phased out in later years) and the Chiswick cream relief colour round the upper saloon windows.
Clarence Carter/ML

Leatherhead garage received its first RTs in August 1948, being the third country garage after Tring and Hemel Hempstead to be so favoured. RT 633 was one of LH's original batch, arriving in September 1948, and is seen here in 1959. By this stage, the Aldenham overhaul system was in full swing and this bus is not exactly the same vehicle as the original one of that fleet number. During the life of the RTs various changes were introduced and several can be seen in this photograph when compared to that of RT 1023; the cream upper-deck window surrounds are now green, the polished wheel embellishers are painted, the headlamps and fog lamps have been replaced by the larger style, a steel plate is used to blank off the bottom of the radiator, and flashing direction indicators have been fitted. The latter had been introduced experimentally in 1956 on a small number of vehicles but in 1958 it was announced that the entire fleet would be equipped with indicators of a revised design, work which was mainly carried out in 1959. RT 633 is seen at Chessington Zoo in August.
Ian Stewart/ML

RT 3639 works a 152, Feltham to Mitcham, in 1958, the year of the disastrous bus strike in which the staff and the operator lost income and the passengers, in many cases, found alternative methods of travel and did not return to bus ridership, so this picture of a bus surrounded by private cars is somewhat prophetic. The scene is Bushy Park and the cars as well as the bus would be collectible today. *Phil Tatt/ML*

Left Lazy blinds were not really a good use of LT's excellent destination displays but there were several examples. RT 291 shows one such on the first day of operation of the 263. Unusually, the conductor is collecting fares from potential passengers before they board because the large queue and short route would make it virtually impossible to do so when the bus got under way. LT made it clear that a conductor's duty was to collect every fare and to ensure it was correct, with no over-riding. A contemporary booklet, 'How to Conduct a Bus', indicates that if one 2d fare went uncollected on every journey, LT would lose £250,000 per annum, a staggering sum. *Prince Marshall/ML*

Above London Transport's master plan for the post-war fleet was to have completely standardised vehicles which could be driven, maintained and overhauled with ease and it intended therefore to buy many thousands of identical buses. Shortages of materials and skilled workers in the immediate post-war period, however, meant that deliveries of new vehicles were frequently disrupted and older vehicles were becoming unserviceable at a faster rate than new ones could be supplied. Several solutions to this problem were tried and one was to buy bodies from additional contractors. One such was the Sheffield-based Cravens Railway Carriage and Wagon Company. Despite its title, this firm also built bus bodies and supplied 120 of its standard design on RT chassis. The latter, unlike most chassis, came without front bulkhead, bonnet and wings and Cravens had to modify the body to incorporate these components, together with the standard RT cab, but otherwise the design was the same as that supplied on AEC chassis to Sheffield Corporation and Guy Arab to Scotland's W. Alexander empire. The Cravens buses began to arrive in 1948 and were supplied to both central and country departments. The latter confined their examples to Windsor and Watford High Street garages, but the red buses were scattered around the fleet in small numbers. Their bodies had nothing in common with any other RT-family design, and keeping spare parts for 120 buses was not considered economically worthwhile, so between 1955 and 1957 the entire batch was withdrawn and sold. This seems wasteful, but relatively young buses which had been well maintained would fetch a good price and this was deemed preferable to retaining them. RT 1519, delivered in 1950, is working a 38 from Leyton garage (T). This bus did not move far from London when sold, passing to Red Rover of Aylesbury who removed its roof box and ran it until December 1966. *Geoff Morant/ML*

Prior to main-line railway electrification, the east London Green Line services into Minories Coach Station at Aldgate were very popular and had been operated by double-deck vehicles for some years to cope with demand. In August 1950 Romford garage received RTs 3224-3259 to replace wartime utility Daimlers and a handful of STLs on the 721 Brentwood–Aldgate, the 722 Upminster–Aldgate and the summer-only 726 Romford–Whipsnade services. Mechanically and bodily these buses were no different from other RTs, but they were finished in Green Line colours of Lincoln green with light green relief, carried Green Line fleet names and an impressive cast-aluminium bullseye motif, and were devoid of commercial advertising, thus setting them apart from the rest of the RT fleet. RT 3224 is seen at Aldgate shortly after entering service. Note the original-style Green Line blinds and the two rexine radiator blinds in the rolled up position; these quickly became tatty in service and were subsequently replaced by metal plates, painted black. In 1959 the Green Line RTs became the first of their class to be equipped with saloon heaters.
Don Jones/ML

Romford garage operated no bus services so its Green Line RTs were not officially allocated to any bus routes. The vehicles were however occasionally loaned to garages within the same engineering group to cover a shortage, especially during the period when the summer 726 was not operating and it had more than enough spares. Here at Hoddesdon clock tower in 1956 we see one such loan, in this case RT 3225. *Alan B Cross collection/ML*

Below This delightfully rural scene – not unlike that to be seen in many an English village – is the centre of Pinner. No sign of any cars, yellow lines, street clutter, or indeed people. Where is everyone? The scene – possibly early sixties though more typical of the fifties – strongly suggests Sunday and the position of the sun tells us it is lunchtime, so perhaps the crew have gone for a bite to eat if their layover time here permitted this. Peter Stuyvesant cigarettes, advertised on the side of the RT, came to Britain in the fifties as an upmarket alternative to Woodbines, Player's Navy Cut or Weights, while Battersea fun fair was a legacy from the Festival of Britain. RT 910 was allocated to Hendon garage in September 1959 following an overhaul that gave it an RT3 body. It was one of those to end up being sold to the Ceylon Transport Board, to whom it went at the end of 1964.

London Transport began to introduce 'Express' buses in the 1950s in an attempt to improve journey times and attract increased custom. The entire exercise was conducted in a somewhat sporadic and patchy way in both central and country areas, but some such services were run successfully for a number of years. Express buses normally (but not invariably) featured destination blinds with a blue background rather than the normal black. A popular way to spend a day out in the 1950s and 1960s, particularly after the introduction of Rover tickets in 1957, was to take a bus to a tourist attraction such as Hampton Court, London Airport (really!) or Windsor. The latter was a particular favourite with its Castle and royal connections, a number of interesting historic buildings and the River Thames with pleasure steamers and private-hire boats. The first 457 expresses from Uxbridge ran at Easter, Whitsun and Sundays from 15th July 1956, and stopped only at the terminal points and Windsor High Street (opposite the Castle). The service ceased in October 1956 for the winter but reappeared in subsequent years. Why was it so popular? Uxbridge was a focal point for country area buses from Hemel Hempstead, St Albans, Garston, Luton, etc, central area buses from several places (and trolleybus 607 from Shepherds Bush) and a terminus of the Metropolitan and Piccadilly Underground lines. It was served by another Express bus, too – the 803 from Welwyn Garden City – so a great many passengers for Windsor travelled via Uxbridge and the 457. RT 3505 is seen at the aforementioned High Street stop, returning to Uxbridge very lightly loaded. The bus has a roof-box body of the type that was to become classified RT10. These had the lower cab front panel modified so that such bodies could be fitted to RTL chassis as well as RT. The canopy shroud has a reduced depth and a holder is fitted to the front bulkhead for the route number plate in the same position as the roller blind on RT3/1 and subsequent bodies – compare this with the photo of RT 633. The Aldenham system resulted in many earlier bodies emerging from overhaul with high fleet numbers and, conversely, some much newer bodies were turned out with very low numbers. *Alan B Cross collection/ML*

The popularity of weekend bus and Green Line trips often put a great strain on the Country Bus and Coach Department and all available vehicles were pressed into service. To cope with demand, it was the practice to borrow red buses from suitably-located garages to operate extra journeys. An earlier shot than that of RT 3505 is this evocative study of red RT 2138 crossing Windsor Bridge with the Castle in the background. The bus is on loan to Windsor from Uxbridge and shows the practice of setting the blinds to black blanks and sticking a paper bill with the route number and brief details of places served onto the glass. At the rear, a similar process took place but the bills were stuck to the lower saloon back window, avoiding the work of changing blinds when a bus was loaned for just day or a weekend. *Peter Grace/ML*

Seen at Corbets Tey on 3rd August 1958 are Upton Park's RT 3314, about to work an 86 to Limehouse, and RT 430 on the short local service to Upminster. The latter vehicle was originally a roof-box bus but following overhaul now has a later-style body. This short route was one of a small number to make use of so-called 'lazy' blinds which did not require changing at each end of the route. Standing alongside is a Green Line RT awaiting its next run to Aldgate. *Alan B Cross collection/ML*

Above right A 'Hop on a Bus' advertising campaign began in November 1958, after the strike, in an endeavour to win back some passengers lost at the time. These were dark days for LT and many services were reduced in frequency or abandoned, while buses began to be sold off in increasing quantities, although this latter move did at least permit the stored, brand-new buses to start entering service. Plumstead's RT 2175, awaiting its next turn on the 122 in January 1959, displays its hop-inviting posters. *Phil Tatt/ML*

Right As it said on the 'Private' blinds, you could always hire a bus (or coach), although LT was to become unenthusiastic about the practice in the light of persistent staff shortages. This delightful period shot of two RTs – 2527 and another – in Gravel Hill, Addington, illustrates such a private hire; the buses are from Croydon garage and are carrying cub scouts to Baden Powell's Gilwell Scout Camp in north London. PSV Regulations at that time allowed three children (there was an upper age limit) to occupy the space normally taken up by two adults. The lack of traffic and the motorcycle combination are both of note. *Terry Russell/ML*

Another solution to the new bus shortage was to buy chassis from another supplier. Only Leyland Motors had sufficient capacity to assist, but their range did not include a model with fluid transmission, and given that LT wanted complete interchangeability of bodies, a further problem was that their PD2 chassis did not match the exact dimensions and profile of the AEC Regent 3RT. In the event and after much negotiation, what happened was one of the most interesting and unusual events ever to take place in the British motor industry. A major manufacturer with its own highly successful range of vehicles, sold at home and overseas, built a large number of chassis which were in essence a copy of another manufacturer's product. Furthermore, that other manufacturer was also a successful, market-leading concern and Leyland's biggest rival. Nothing like this had happened before or is ever likely to again, but Leyland Motors agreed to build chassis based on the RT, incorporating fluid flywheel, gearbox, gear selector and handbrake mechanisms supplied by AEC, and with air, electrical and chassis lubrication systems made by proprietary concerns and as fitted to the RT, but unlike those habitually used by Leyland. Leyland engine, radiator, suspension, steering gear and axles, however, were included. The resulting bus was the RTL. Here is a very early colour shot of RTL 128 in Whitehall in as-delivered condition working London's best-known bus route, the 11. This bus was a February 1949 delivery. *W.J. Wyse/ML*

Left RTL 1044, new in September 1950 to Athol Street (Poplar) garage, is seen here in revised livery without cream upper-deck windows but still with restricted blind display, and is in front of a sister bus fitted with Metro-Cammell bodywork, another instance of an additional supplier becoming involved to speed deliveries. 450 Metro-Cammell bodies were fitted to RTL chassis only and were not interchangeable with the products of other builders. The 'all-red' livery had begun to appear on new RTLs in April 1950. *Don Jones/ML*

The RTLs were a very good attempt to produce a Lancashire-built RT, but they exhibited characteristics that made them less popular than their AEC counterparts. The first was an erratic tickover which caused problems with vibrations when idling and caused surging when pulling away. John A Gray recollects "waiting for a crew change at Church Road, Hanwell, while the brand new RTL stood at the kerbside, engine ticking over. Well, not so much ticking, but shaking … enough even for my father to notice, 'it's as bad as those other new buses we had a year or two back', meaning the post-war STDs. He would have suggested a firing order of 1-5-3-6-2-4 followed by a whistling breather before repeating." Respected photographer Alan B Cross has similar memories: "I am afraid I never quite took to them. My first ride on a brand new one was on the 137 and when idling at stops it was most uncomfortable. The body shook and we were shaken up with it. This was quite a familiar experience for a while and most noticeable when sitting upstairs." The second characteristic was heavier steering than the AECs. RT front axles took the weight of the bus by means of roller bearings at the bottom end of the king-pins, and these are almost friction-free. Leyland, in contrast, favoured the simpler (and cheaper) 'thrust button'. In this system, the king-pin has a hollowed-out recess which fits over a domed (and replaceable) button which is not as free-moving as a roller bearing. This led to heavier steering on the RTLs (though not as heavy as on RTWs). It must be said, however, that the lubrication was critical and there was a vast difference between a well oiled Leyland and a dry one. Steering wheel shake was another feature of the Leylands that made them less popular with drivers. Finally, there was the gearchange, which was slower than that of the RTs. Leon Daniels remembers that "a smooth gearchange took rather longer on an RTL or RTW than on an RT. Partially because of the erratic tickover and 'hunting', engine revs died away more slowly. If you attempted operation of the gear change pedal at 'AEC' speeds the transmission gave you a little push and all the passengers a mild whiplash. A smooth Leyland gearchange became like a pilot's coveted 'greased' landing – delivered only by professionals". This interesting historic photograph of RTL 1114 shows it alongside prototype Routemaster RM 1, a vehicle which, with power steering fitted in 1956 and automatic transmission, would not suffer from the defects ascribed to the Leyland. In the condition depicted, RM 1 normally worked the 2 on weekends for some two years from March 1957. The RTL has been fitted with the brackets for trafficators (the original design, not perpetuated, of these "ears" is shown on the RM), so we can deduce that this photograph dates from early 1959.
Alan B Cross collection/ML

It is ironic that notwithstanding LT's desperate efforts to obtain new vehicles, even abandoning the idea of complete standardisation, finally it transpired that too many new vehicles had been ordered. The last RTs and RTLs arrived in 1954 but 144, including 63 RTLs, went directly into store where they would remain for up to five years. In March 1958 RTL 1573 emerged to start work at West Green, entering service devoid of external advertising, as shown. The previous month, higher-numbered sister RTL 1618 entered service from Shepherd's Bush in similar external order. This bus has been equipped with trafficators, unlike its sister.
Prince Marshall/ML

The intention had been to build an 8-foot wide version of the RT, to be coded 4RT4, but in the event Leyland Motors were also awarded the contract for these wider buses. The RTW class, 500-strong, had a wider version of the RTL chassis with different axles to suit but this time, since body interchangeability with the rest of the RT family was not possible, Leyland also built the bodies. Using their standard patented method of construction, they produced an excellent 'RT look-alike' and probably most casual passers-by did not realise these buses were quite different from other RT types. RTW 168 stands in the company of RTW 459 at Willesden garage as the last traces of March 1958 snow melt away. *Ron Copson/ML*

Conducting and Driving

John Churchman

My mate 'Bo' Smith had been a trolleybus conductor at Holloway depot for some time, and when I was looking for a new job, in the second half of 1949, he suggested that I might like working for London Transport in this capacity. Having been accepted for a position of conductor, I went through the mandatory training period whereby some of the time was spent at Chiswick training centre with the rest of it working with a conductor/instructor at Chalk Farm garage (which was coded CF) – this was the location to which I had been appointed. Having been approved as a conductor I was given a Public Service Vehicle badge, N36899. I was 22 years of age and bus driving was not an option at that time for anyone under 25. When I joined at Chalk Farm most of the buses were STLs, but the garage had very recently received a batch of SRTs for route 24 (Hampstead Heath to Pimlico). The other routes operated were the 3 (Camden Town to Crystal Palace), 31 (Camden Town to Chelsea), 39 (Camden Town to Southfields), and 68 (Chalk Farm to South Croydon). The 68 was a very long route and passed through tram territory in south London. The fares were a bit confusing for where we ran over the same section as trams we had to use their fare scale. We also did summer season weekend work on route 74 shorts between Camden Town and London Zoo. This was a 'bit of corn' (busman's lingo for working some overtime or a day off). If the day had started off fine and then rain came on, inspectors would tell us to run the buses into the garage as there would be nobody wanting to go to the Zoo when it was wet. This was known as a 'storm bus'. We still got paid for this and just went home early. We also operated the summer Sunday extension of route 27 to Hampton Court (its normal weekday terminus was Twickenham). On the earliest trips, a number of fishermen were carried as they reckoned that angling was good

John Churchman in his conducting days with a driver colleague on the left. They are at the Pimlico terminus of route 24 in front of SRT 100. *John Churchman collection*

on the River Thames there. Later on, the bus would fill up on fine days as people took the opportunity of visiting Hampton Court Palace. We had to go through Bushy Park where deer could be seen – a far cry from urban Camden Town. Good loads were carried on some of the later buses to leave Hampton Court and often our final trip from 'The Court' would be the last of the day. To use the old boys' expression, the drivers would 'put the coals on' so that we could get back to CF a bit early – but not enough to attract an inspector's attention!

A 'rookie' conductor on the 24s had to learn a couple of matters very quickly as I found out – both at Pimlico; it was all to do with the terminal arrangements there. Number one: from Lupus Street, the 24 turned left into Westmoreland Terrace from where it turned left again to stand in Grosvenor Road – it returned via Claverton Street to regain Lupus Street. Some passengers who got off at the terminus would board a 24 that was waiting there and travel on it to their stop on the loop, considering this to be a continuation of their journey. Number two: some of those living there treated the 24 as a free service – they'd board it wherever they wanted so that they could get to the George IV pub. Both were accepted practices by the staff for the locals and I had to fall in with them.

Ticket issuing equipment at the start of the 1950s comprised a rack of pre-printed tickets of different colours and a machine that punched holes in the appropriate fare stage the passenger had paid for. A bell rang when the ticket was punched and the machine had a container at the bottom that collected the 'confetti' from the punched tickets in case a count was needed back at the garage. It was a more time consuming process than the use of the Gibson ticket-issuing machine that came in later in the decade, but conductors managed. An example of where collecting all the fares was virtually impossible was the section of the 24 between Pimlico and Victoria in the morning rush hour. This part of the journey took seven minutes and I would often have a bus full of passengers, almost all of whom wanted to get off at Victoria. A full load was 61 (including five standing in the lower deck). It was all I could do to get round the lower deck in this time; if I had not had to give out too much change I might be able to get in some of the top deck fares – starting at the back meant that those who hadn't yet paid had to come past me. They'd bung money into my hands and I'd just punch off the relevant number of tickets at Victoria. If I hadn't been able to start collecting from the top deck, the money would be thrust into my hands on the platform – again punch off tickets equivalent to the money given to me. Going back the other way in the evening was not so bad as people had different finishing times. The highest number of tickets I issued in one day was about a thousand. I never got to use a Gibson because by the time they came in I was a driver. The old pennies (or 'coppers' as we called them) were quite heavy and I was provided with a leather shoulder bag to carry these and also the smaller quantity of silver that was collected. So many copper coins were proffered that, having put them in copper bags, I placed them in a locker which was beneath the stairs and secured by a budget key. All staff had to wear a uniform which was supplied to us; despite the trousers being made of serge, the continual brushing past the seats took the hair off my legs. I very much enjoyed the job and always gave my best.

Not all bus crews were looking to issue record numbers of tickets. There were all sorts of ploys that some would use to have a quieter life. These tricks mostly involved somehow getting immediately behind another bus and following it as far as they could so that the first bus picked up all the passengers. Going around Parliament Square or Trafalgar Square twice was one of the ruses used occasionally to swap places with a bus behind. Another was to act as though the bus had broken down, until it miraculously worked again after being passed by another. The drivers tried these ruses mostly when they had women conductors, as they wanted to give them an easy time. Sometimes the conductresses themselves would play a trick. Rose, a Chalk Farm conductress, when at the stop opposite the Bedford Theatre in Camden High Street on a route 24 bus, was known to change the rear blind to 68 to lure the driver of a 29, 39 or 134 to go in front. Having succeeded she would change the blind back to 24. In my first couple of years as a conductor, restricted 'wartime' blinds were in use because of a shortage of material. Only one blind was used at the back; this was the top one and I had to undo a flap, put my hand inside the blind box and change the blind to the appropriate display. The front display had the same configuration; with my budget key I opened the blind box housing and wound the destination blind round. Most of the trips were Pimlico to Hampstead Heath and vice-versa so it was only one rotation of the handle. Later on, when more material was available and buses had blinds in all apertures, the driver changed the front destination blind. Only thirty-nine minutes was allowed, each way, on the 24 route, although in the peak hour it was increased to forty-four.

Continuing the theme of not picking up too many passengers – or any at all! Routes 24, 29, 39 and 134 followed the same line of route between Camden Town and Victoria; whoever came up first at Camden Road on this section took all 'the rabbits' – busman's jargon for those jumping on a bus at the last minute. Each bus would push the other all the way – 'right up his staircase' as we would put it. The 24s and the 134s were the greatest rivals as they both went to Pimlico. The 134s were run by Potters Bar and Holloway garages, while the 24 was operated by Chalk Farm – the fact that crews from different garages had to pick up passengers on the same roads caused the friction. The worst scenes happened on the last buses on the 24s and 134s – there were some very angry crews sometimes. This was because the last 134 was supposed to be three minutes in front of the last 24, and of course the 134 would arrive late in the hope that the 24 would take all the passengers on this last but very busy trip – it was no good the last 24 arriving late as if he did catch a load, it could be difficult to get back to the garage on time. Difficulties also arose at Pimlico itself, due to the fact that these two routes had different termini there. The 24s ended their journeys at Grosvenor Road, while the 134s finished at Dolphin Square, where many la-di-dah people lived. This meant that the 134s had the advantage over the 24s in that they could see us go by while they waited in Claverton Street.

Sometimes sporting fixtures made things easier. For example, when Chelsea was playing at home, we would fill up a 31 at Camden Town and I would have all the way to Chelsea's ground to collect the fares. No-one got off so no-one else got on. We would get complaints from people about not stopping at bus stops to pick them up, but we couldn't; we were full. Because it skirted central London, the 31 at other times was quite a hard route to conduct because it was a 'fast road' and we had to work quickly to keep up. It was nicknamed 'the wall of death' by the crews.

I was conducting on the 24s on Coronation day (2nd June 1953). Chalk Farm garage ran only as far as Warren Street – we turned round in Maple Street where the trolleybuses terminated; the middle part of the route was unserved as it went through the Coronation route. From Victoria to Pimlico, the 24 was operated by STD buses from Gillingham Street garage. Aware that people wanted to travel into central London early to get a good position along the Coronation route to see the procession, some very early buses were run. The first 24 left Hampstead Heath at 4.11am and by 6.30 passenger loadings were similar

Chalk Farm's RTW 180 on the 'wall of death' route 31, which received RTWs in the autumn of 1950 after the Metropolitan Police had been convinced that the extra six inches' width would not cause a problem in central London. *Alan B Cross*

to peak hours. Because it was only about a twenty minute run between 'The Heath' and Maple Street, I made loads of trips and paid in lots of money that day. The 24s and 31s were the busiest routes from Chalk Farm garage, operating to low frequency headways. Therefore there tended to be bunching of buses and inspectors tried with varying degrees of success to keep buses spaced out and in the right order, e.g. CF27 was to be followed by CF28. However, when buses were completely full there was no point to this and, when working on the 24, inspectors would sometimes sign our log cards (which were a record of our trips) with the letters ATP which meant 'Authority to Pass' – that meant 'jump' the bus in front. This meant that if another inspector was to ask why we were running early and out of order, we were exonerated. Inspectors on the 31 worked differently and would not participate in this practice. The STLs were showing their age by the time I started, and rattled like chicken houses, but were still good mechanically. The SRTs in comparison had very quiet bodywork, though they had other shortcomings which I will come to later when I move on to my driving days. Only a few busmen at the garage owned a car in those days, but some had motorbikes on which they could get to work. There was also a night-time and early morning network of staff buses to get bus (and Underground) workers to and from work where no service buses were running. I moved over to driving when I reached the age of 25 in 1953. All tuition was from the Chiswick training school based within the grounds of the works and took about three weeks to complete. This was at a time when very few trainees had experience of driving even a car. For my part, I'd only used a push bike and now London Transport were teaching me to drive a double-deck bus for which I would receive a full council driving licence in the process. The vehicle I and many others trained on was a pre-selector STL – a system similar to that on the RTs but with a floor mounted gear stick instead of the column-mounted design on the RT family.

The Chiswick skid pan was the best part of the instruction. An old STL which had the window between the cab and saloon removed was used. On the first run, towards an area that was continually sprayed with water, the instructor got me to go as fast as I could towards the water and got me to stop ordinarily. Before I started the second run (at the same speed) he told me that he was going to yank the handbrake on; this would show what happened if we did this on an icy road. The bus turned nearly 180 degrees, swaying all over the place, coming to a halt almost in the opposite direction. With two or three more runs I was really getting into it and he told me that each time he pulled the steering wheel I should turn into the skid – this straightened the bus up. The skid pan was directly in front of some offices and no bus ever went into them – I wonder what those who worked there regularly thought about having a bus heading towards them at a crazy angle. I got more confidence from twenty minutes on the skid pan than the three weeks of learning in normal conditions. It was a bit nerve-racking on the first couple of runs, but was great fun. This was all done at the end of the training course when drivers were used to a bus.

Chiswick was also the starting point for the driving test. London Transport had its own ministry-approved examiners, and Mr Poyle took me for my test. He was known as the toughest examiner there and always took candidates up Chancery Lane. It was a tight left turn from High Holborn into Chancery Lane which was a narrow street that was still two-way in those days. He must have thought I was competent as he passed me at my first attempt. I was given Public Service Vehicle badge N41467.

I lived a ten-minute walk away from Chalk Farm and so was always punctual. Probably because of this, when I was on early turn, I was sometimes given the first 68 duty – this was because the scheduled driver was still in bed! When we had them, this was always an STL even after the route was converted to RTL (which took place in the latter part of 1950). The reason for this was probably due to the fact that the running number that the bus was on stayed in the garage for most of the day after its trip back from South Croydon, leaving the rest of the route to the newer buses. Taking out an STL first thing on a cold winter morning is an experience never forgotten. They had no cab door and the driving cab would be very, very cold – especially if there was a wind blowing in across Waterloo Bridge. I used to put cycle clips on my trousers to protect me from the drafts coming up through the floor. By the time I was a driver, the only route to be allocated any STLs at the garage was the 74, which used them on the summer supplementary Saturday shorts between the Zoo and Camden Town. We had a handful of STLs for this and for general spares.

Earlier I briefly mentioned the SRTs – STL chassis temporarily fitted with RT bodies. The engine, gearbox and all the other gubbins was from the STL, but the gear selector unit on the steering column was of the RT type. Because the RT bodies were over half a ton heavier than the STL ones, the braking was not quite what it should be. A lot of extra care was needed therefore when driving an SRT and London Transport soon learned that the buses needed to be put on routes free of steep hills. Apart from the 24, Chalk Farm also used SRTs on new route 196, introduced in October 1950, and this kept them until it was extended from Waterloo to Norwood Junction the following July, when it was converted to RTL. The SRTs also suffered from poor acceleration, again because of the body weight and this could make it difficult to keep up with the schedule at times. Even in the 1950s, wood blocks were still to be seen. One place where they were still used was in Charing Cross Road and if it had been raining when going towards Pimlico, I had to drive very gingerly to avoid sliding on them. There was a general air of unhappiness among the driving staff about these buses and they had to be driven with great caution. I remember once, when the SRT that I had been driving on the 24 broke down at Pimlico, I was given an RT from Victoria garage in exchange (this garage worked the 24s on Sundays, so were fitted with blinds for this route). I had to work it back in service, but without realising it I continued to drive as though it was an SRT, with the result that the

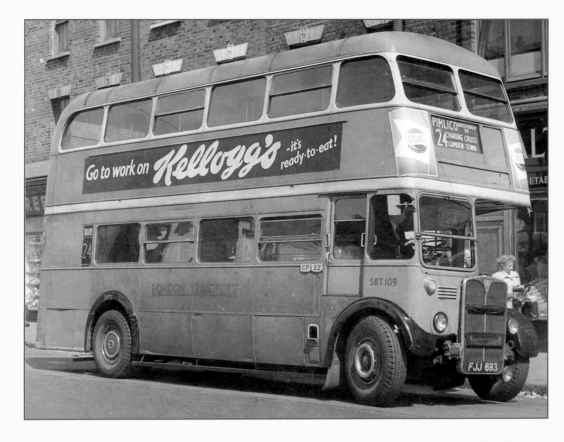

SRT 109 is seen in Camden High Street. Route 24 was selected as one of the routes suitable for these vehicles owing to the lack of steep gradients along it. *Prince Marshall*

speed I was doing up Whitehall attracted the attention of a police motorcyclist; I must have been doing about 35mph, when all buses were restricted to 30. He followed me to Leicester Square but gave up on me by the time I reached Cambridge Circus due to the amount of traffic in the area. In all my years on the job, I never got booked by an inspector – more by luck than judgement! However, I did get reported by a 'Whitehall Warrior'; our term for men with pinstripe trousers, a black coat, bowler hat and a rolled up umbrella. I was driving up Whitehall towards Trafalgar Square when a man waved his brolly; as I wasn't at a stop, I thought he was hailing a taxi. I wasn't going to slam my brakes on for somebody who might want my 24 and thought no more about it. A few days later I was called in to see the chief depot inspector – this fellow had noted down the registration number of the bus and written to London Transport complaining that I hadn't stopped for him. I told the CDI my version of events – he was satisfied with my explanation and the matter was dropped.

Compared with the SRTs (and the RTs that I drove when I later moved to Edgware) the RTLs had heavier steering and were noisier in the cab – these arrived in May 1950 for use on the 31 route. RTWs were also allocated to Chalk Farm (from the autumn of 1950); they were six inches wider than the RTs and RTLs and were mostly to be seen on routes 31 and 39. They had even heavier steering and sometimes I had to half stand up in the cab to turn an RTW's steering wheel on a tight corner. On one occasion, one almost completely seized up and I could not get it to turn left. When I phoned the garage, I don't think they believed me. A Divisional Mechanical Inspector came down to the bus – a man of this rank only attended to reports of very serious problems. He also could not turn the bus left, and in the end had to find a way back to the garage using a rather long route that took right turns and straights only; he went all over the place to get the bus home. I made my own way back to Chalk Farm and heard about his circuitous journey later. The extra six inches width of the RTWs also made quite a difference to the driver. On their first morning out with them, some drivers did minor damage to the nearside roof dome by hitting lamp posts in Adelaide Road. We had a bit of type training on them but not much. Between Camden Town and Victoria, SRT route 24 paralleled RTW route 39 and it was always more difficult to get through the traffic in an RTW, which could also be seen on the 24s and 68s at times. There was a short time in 1954 when Chalk Farm operated RT, RTL, RTW and SRT buses simultaneously – it was the only location in the fleet where this occurred. This happened when they were getting rid of the SRTs – once the engineers had decided to withdraw them, matters moved very quickly, and the RTs were a stop-gap measure until enough RTLs were available. The last SRTs went in June 1954 and all the drivers were pleased to see the back of them. To sum up my driving days at Chalk Farm, the AEC RTs and SRTs were far better to drive than the Leyland RTLs and RTWs. In fact the RTLs and RTWs were heavier and noisier than the much maligned SRTs.

Some inspectors had nicknames. One was 'Wanna Buy a Watch?'. Based at Trafalgar Square as a Silver Badge Inspector, he was well-liked and was promoted to Gold Badge at some stage. He would carry a large selection of wrist-watches hanging on safety pins inside his overcoat, and would often greet us with his invitation to buy a watch. Drivers and conductors had their own traits and there were many colourful characters in the garage. My first driver rolled his own cigarettes with Boar's Head tobacco. He gave me one once – it was horrible black stuff and terribly strong; I didn't try it again. London busmen are famed for their liking of tea and many have been booked by inspectors over the years for arriving early at a terminus where there was a canteen. In my opinion the best place in the fleet to get a cup of tea was at Crystal Palace where route 3 terminated; there was a green refreshment hut and the ladies there gave us a marvellous cuppa. It may have been the water that was used along with the London Transport Griffin tea.

I transferred to Edgware (coded EW) in the latter part of 1958. The only types here were RTs and single-deck TDs. I needed to take further training for the crash gearboxes on the TDs, as did any driver moving from a garage that did not have them; I had to go to Chiswick where I had a couple of day's training. The crash gearbox was a complex unit to master, so a stringent procedure meant that although I was officially only doing type training, I had to be approved to drive them. I was again taken out by Mr Poyle who was still a strict examiner all those years later. Again, he made me do the tight left turn from High Holborn into Chancery Lane. In fact I missed a gear change on the test and he said to me "Who passed you out?" I replied "You did sir!" The TDs were used on route 240A between Edgware station and Mill Hill East, and tended to be worked by the older drivers who had begun their driving careers on such gearboxes – the route was known as 'the old man's road'. They were hard work and a lot of the younger drivers really hated them. I had to double de-clutch between each gear change, though I could always get away without this between first and second when the lever had to be pulled back about two feet. The 240A was a short route with lots of corners and hills; the steering was hard work and the vehicles had a heavy clutch, so by the end of a day spent on the 240A, my arms and legs could ache quite a lot. About half the service only worked as far as Mill Hill Broadway, and there was a Sunday duty that did eighteen trips between Edgware and the Broadway – eleven journeys first half, seven journeys second half. Not popular at all. Upon the closure of Colindale trolleybus depot in January 1962, some of their staff transferred to Edgware. Most of their drivers were frightened of the TDs, and when booked up to work some extra time on them would try to get rid of the duty to someone else. However, 'old man Collins' relished the challenge as he'd driven virtually anything that moved – trams, trolleybuses, motorbuses, cars, lorries, bikes, etc. For most of the Colindale drivers it must have been a world apart, driving a trolleybus and then driving a crash gearbox TD.

There was no opportunity to get up a good speed for very long on a 240A; the only time that I could let a TD out was when I used one on the night-time staff bus that left Edgware to travel all the way to Upney, principally taking Underground railway staff home. No route learning was given and I had to find my way. On the first day I got to Maida Vale and there was a railwayman waiting who wanted to go most of the way; I invited him up into the cab where he sat on the regulator box and guided me through central London and onto Bow Road. Various members of the train staff were picked up at Underground stations or a nearby point. The meal relief was at Camberwell garage; after that, it was back to Barking to pick up staff who were now going to work. This time the bus came down the East India Dock Road and Commercial Road before travelling through central London and along the Edgware Road back to EW. The bus was available to any member of staff and I picked up people who were travelling to Cricklewood bus garage and Colindale trolleybus depot as well as my home garage. I drove this rail-staff bus a few times, and soon found out that there were members of the public who were using it! These were newspaper staff who worked in Fleet Street and who would board at Aldgate; on alighting, some would give me a newspaper. I accepted that this was just one of those things that went on, but when Bert Ensor first did the duty, he was a bit put out that all he got was a paper; these men were earning good money and he thought that he should have a financial reward. He told the men that he would take them on the first night but would expect something more thereafter. This put a stop to the practice and whenever I did the duty afterwards there were no free newspapers as the men had all made other travel arrangements. Eventually the TGWU put a block on the rail-bus as it took a driver off a duty and meant some journeys would not run due to staff shortage.

Fog has always been an occupational hazard for bus drivers and it brings to mind incidents at Hampstead Heath. Upon leaving, trolleybuses headed down Constantine Road before turning slightly left, and down Agincourt Road; as it was not an obvious turn some drivers missed it and carried on down Constantine Road. Trolley arms flew off the wires and crews had a bit of a palaver sorting things out and reversing the vehicles back on battery. When it was really foggy, I could only see six inches in front of me; my eyes would be out on stalks and streaming. It was so bad one night that my conductor and I, when we were working on a 107 (mentioned in the next paragraph), stayed at Ponders End for hours before the fog lifted and I was able to see the road ahead.

Driving from Edgware was very different to driving from Chalk Farm. On my first day there, I arrived at Edgware from Watford on the 142 ten minutes early; the inspector on duty went mad. I explained to him that it was my first day working in the suburbs and I wasn't used to the quiet road conditions – he just advised me. As I had a lot of seniority to my credit, I was put on to the 107 rota virtually straight away. The 107 ran from Queensbury to Ponders End on weekdays, with a 107A operating on a Sunday between Edgware and Enfield Lock. This route had RTs which were luxurious compared to the vehicles I had driven at Chalk Farm.

It was the same old games at Edgware as at Chalk Farm – crews on different routes trying to get one over on each other. The 142 joined the 158 at Bushey 'Alpine'; the 142 had come across Stanmore Common from Edgware, while the 158 had come up Common Road from Harrow Weald. Drivers on both routes would go slowly up to the traffic lights, hoping that the opposition would materialise. That was on the northern section of the 142; on the southern section of the route, between Edgware and Cricklewood, the same tricks were played between the 142s and the trolleybuses – the 142s could get caught out as the trolleybus staff sometimes changed over outside Colindale depot. This meant that the 142s had to 'take the road' because changeovers weren't always immediate and they couldn't sit behind a trolleybus in the meantime. The same scenarios also happened on the 107, for Country Bus route 306 which ran between New Barnet and Leavesden, paralleled the 107 between New Barnet and Elstree. This was a mighty long way, and whichever came up first at either Elstree or New Barnet got all the passengers. The RTs were a driver's bus and the best I ever drove.

The two photos on this page provide a good comparison between the Weymann bodied post-war TDs and the Mann Egerton ones. The photo above can also be compared with that of the Weymann bodied T on page 16: the Weymann body is a happier fit on the Leyland chassis than on the AEC. TD 25, seen in Kingston, was one of 31 similar vehicles delivered in the latter part of 1946 and the early part of 1947. The Mann Egerton ones began to arrive about a year later. Whereas the latter lasted in London service until October 1962, Ts 1-31 had all gone by March 1958. *LRTA*

Below and right The one hundred Mann Egerton bodied TDs bought in 1948/9 lasted much longer with London Transport than might have been expected for non-standard vehicles, and from the latter part of 1955 through to their final demise in 1962 the TDs were the only crash gearbox vehicles in the Central Bus fleet. In their later careers many drivers – now totally accustomed to preselector gearboxes – began to dislike and, in a few cases, even fear driving them. By the time that TD 103 was photographed arriving at Uxbridge it had received an earlier style, chromium plated, Leyland radiator from the first TD series (TD 1-31) instead of its polished aluminium original, whilst Kingston's TD 88 had been modified to the extent that the nearside route stencil plate had been moved from above the doorway to a new position below the front window, presumably for the ease of garage staff. *Peter Grace, Prince Marshall/KB*

RLH 13 lays over at Amersham Station in 1956 while working on route 359 to Aylesbury. The driver, who is keeping a stern eye on his charge, has placed a wheel scotch against the offside front wheel as an additional safety measure against the bus running away. Wheel scotches were provided at the time at terminals where the buses stood on a gradient. In addition to the low-bridge route 336, RLHs were allocated to Amersham garage to work routes 305/A and 359 which did not require the low-height type. Route 359 had been introduced in September 1942 when the Green Line route to Aylesbury via Amersham had been withdrawn and was jointly worked between London Transport and United Counties Omnibus Company with each operator providing just one bus. From October 1958 a one-man operated RF replaced the RLH on the route. RLH 13 survived into the London Country period and was withdrawn from Guildford garage in June 1970. *Alan B Cross collection/LA*

New housing development meant that the TD single deckers on route 248 were becoming inadequate to cope with demand. Accordingly on 16th March 1955 RLHs replaced them on the short route from Upminster Hall Lane to Cranham which passed under a low bridge in St Mary's Lane. The RLH was very much a non-standard bus for London Transport, its provincial appearance giving away the fact that it had been designed for a non-London customer. Any passenger of average stature travelling on the upper deck would have a very restricted view of the outside world, as their eye level would have been above the windows. If sitting in the front seat one would get a view of the piece road a few yards in front of the bus. The offside gangway meant that the conductor might have to lean across three other passengers when collecting the fare of the fourth person in the corner seat position. The lower saloon was little better as anyone sitting on the offside below the sunken gangway had a good chance of bumping their head when leaving their seat. The seat frames had curved handrails which were quite different from those found on the RT family. No back blind box was fitted which made them look even more provincial when viewed from the rear. RLH 72 is seen at Upminster station.
Alan B Cross collection/LA

RLH 59 was allocated to Merton from new in December 1952 until its first overhaul in June 1956. This garage needed the low height type for the somewhat circuitous route 127 from Morden to South Wimbledon which went under the bridge at Worcester Park station. The bus is at North Cheam calling at one of the pre-war combined bus and coach stop signs. The little black stickers applied to either side of the bus stop bullseye denote respectively bus and coach fare stage. Similar stickers were applied to all fare stage stop flags as a result of public protestation following the March 1952 fares revision. This revision was particularly severe being in today's parlance a "double whammy" – not only was the general fare scale increased but additional stages were also inserted in to the faretables. Thus for many journeys passengers found themselves facing a double increase. As a result the government of the day directed London Transport to advise passengers of the locations of the fare stages. *Michael Wickham collection/LA*

Class B Clerk at £200 per annum

Ken Blacker

Nostalgia is a wonderful thing, and it gets more potent the older you grow. If, like me, you can intimately recall London Transport in the early nineteen-fifties, it is hard not to be nostalgic. Though the gloss was wearing off a bit, London Transport was still an incredible undertaking with a strong public service ethic and a near monopoly of bus and underground rail services within a radius of some 30 miles from London's centre. To those who worked for it, London Transport could be much more than just a transport provider; it could be a great part of your life if you wanted it to be. It encouraged sports and athletics with excellent grounds at places like Cheam, Walthamstow, Langley Park, Neasden and Osterley. It had a host of off-duty societies and a first rate drama club which staged splendid musicals at a West End theatre. It produced vast quantities of food for staff from its own Food Production Centre at Croydon which, for those who visited it, the enduring memory will always be of seemingly endless strings of newly made sausages, packets of London Transport's own-brand 'Griffin' tea, and 'individual' meat pies. London Transport excelled at Christmas Puddings; theirs were more tasty than you could buy in even the classiest shops. The great organisation even had its own flying club with its own aircraft. It maintained well equipped medical centres dotted around London, and it was so self contained that it even constructed its own ticket punches and printed its own tickets in its works at Effra Road, Brixton. Also – though the old order was beginning to change when I arrived there – London Transport still had a basically stable and loyal workforce which, in many cases, went down through the generations.

This was the London Transport that I applied to join just before leaving school. Having been mad on all forms of public transport for as long as I could remember, London Transport was the only employer I ever thought of working for.

My first visit to 55 Broadway was in response to a letter from E. R. Drake, Staff Officer (who I never met) summoning me to an interview in room 395 at 12.30pm on Friday 13th June – not the most auspicious of dates – 1951. An affable Mr Neale interviewed me and the interview, to my inexperienced mind, was a disaster. I had – or so I kidded myself – a vast knowledge about buses, trams and trains which had accumulated in my mind for years to the almost total exclusion of anything else, and I felt convinced that I could acquit myself well if questioned on any of them. But I wasn't. Instead Mr Neale wanted to discuss the rights and wrongs of the First World War, and the loftier aspects of English Literature's luminaries such as Thomas Hardy and William Blake. The only question vaguely related to transport came right at the end when I was asked whether, if I got the job, I would prefer to work on the railway or road services. I opted for the latter as I thought it offered much wider scope, and then left 55 Broadway with my mind in a state of utter turmoil at such a futile and pointless interview. I walked and walked without noticing where I was going until I found myself on Vauxhall Bridge and finally pulled my thoughts together. Feeling utterly depressed I caught the first tram that came along to Victoria and then an RTL on the 29 home, thinking that perhaps I had better apply to British Railways instead.

Then the letter came, from the same faceless Mr Drake, telling me that, having obtained enough GCE O-Levels, I could start working for London Transport on Monday 20th August 1951 as a Class B Clerk. I had got the job after all on an annual starting salary of £200 paid four-weekly, which was too low to attract tax and produced an income roughly equivalent to £3 16s 10d per week. However it was as much as the big banks were paying a sixteen-year old and the perks were worth having, including heavily subsidised lunches for under eighteens and, more importantly, the cherished piece of coloured card entitling me to travel free on all "London Transport Buses, Trams and Trolleybuses". At that time the Underground was not included although, as a special dispensation, bus staff could use it when on duty or if going to or from work. Free travel throughout the Underground system came not long afterwards, but it took several more years before privilege tickets on British Railways came our way.

I was told to report to the Traffic Development Office which was situated just around the corner from 55 Broadway in a rented building called White Mansions, located in Petty France and made gloomy by a towering and time-blackened Victorian office block known as Queen Anne's Mansions which dominated the scene. All traces of both buildings have long since been obliterated. As a career starting point the Traffic Development Office was an ideal place to be because it had fingers in so many pies. One of its jobs was to control a formidable squad of Loading Reporters, all earthy ex-busmen downgraded for medical reasons, whose job was mainly to stand at bus and tram stops all over the fleet and in all weathers, recording passenger loadings, although on wide headway and country area routes they would generally ride on certain nominated journeys, recording the set-downs and pick-ups at each stop.

At the time of my arrival loadings were being recorded on the remaining tram services prior to their conversion to buses to ascertain that the planned level of replacement buses would be adequate, and the only tram related job I ever did in my career was to check through the incoming loadings to look for possible inadequacies. Being the office boy, I had to look after all the office's huge collection of time schedules which covered the whole fleet, including Country Buses, and which were like an Aladdin's cave of information for me to study avidly in moments of spare time. There was something poignant and final, after each tram conversion, about removing the tram schedules from their drawers and throwing them away.

The Traffic Development Office under its boss G. J. Dickins, a former Country Bus luminary, was part of an empire controlled by the Chief Commercial & Public Relations Officer, and its remit was very wide. It kept an eye on all the new housing and commercial developments going on around London in the early post-war construction boom, which meant plotting maps of new roads, houses and shops on estates such as those at Harold Hill and Ockendon as they went up. The New Towns, such as Crawley and Harlow, had their Development Corporations, but the grandiose expansion plans were still in embryo form in those days. Another facet of the Traffic Development Office's work was to deal with annual renewal of consent to stage carriage operators within London Transport's territory. Most of this was very routine, but the London Passenger Transport Act of 1933 and section 16 (1) of the Transport Act 1947 dictated that every operator had to apply – even if, as in the case of Cole's Blue Bus Service at Windsor, they only ran for as little as half a mile parallel with London Transport's own services.

Much effort was spent organising and running Local Transport Groups which, I was told, were originally a wartime device to co-ordinate transport facilities for factories and to stagger starting and finishing times to make best use of precious transport resources. They were all numbered, 15 for instance being Borehamwood, 22 Silvertown and 27 Mitcham & Hackbridge, but in my immature and naïve view this was all pretty boring stuff compared with the heady development of bus services.

In the office, things that interested the enthusiast just didn't seem to get talked about; indeed the prevailing impression in those days seemed to be that it wouldn't do your career much good to be known as a bus enthusiast. Bus matters were just not on the agenda for everyday chit-chat and only cropped up where the work in hand specifically required it. Of my two closest colleagues at the time – both far older than myself – one only spoke enthusiastically about his dog and his boat moored at Leigh-on-Sea, while the other had a formidable knowledge of personal goings-on, sometimes verging on scandal, and the fluctuating fortunes of Dulwich Hamlet football club. Only many years later did I learn that one quiet, elderly gentleman in the office, who I knew nothing about except that he lived with his sister in Ilford, had actually been interested in buses throughout his career without divulging this information to anyone.

1953 was Coronation year, and I found myself seconded to the Private Hire Department which was then situated on the ground floor at 55 Broadway, just behind the famous trolleybus time recording clocks. There was a huge demand in that year to hire vehicles for private tours of London and my job was to take orders, give quotations and plan itineraries. I was one of a team, several of whom had been doing this job for years. It was a much jollier outfit than the Traffic Development Office, led by an ex-military man who, in *Private Eye* parlance, was usually 'tired and overwrought' each day after a lengthy lunch and was best spoken to in the mornings. However the staff were very loyal and hard working, and although the phones seldom stopped ringing it was a pleasure to work there. The vehicles we hired out consisted mainly of almost new RFs and RFWs, the latter being very comfortable but – in my opinion – some of the ugliest coaches ever built and a great discredit to London Transport's reputation for good design. A substantial minority of hire groups wanted double deckers and to fulfil the demand some of the better time-expired STLs were available for drafting temporarily to garages to cover the private hire orders that we bestowed on them.

After completing two years in the army on compulsory National Service, I returned to the Traffic Development Office in August 1955 to find my job taken by someone else, leaving my unfortunate superiors with the thankless task of finding me odd jobs to do for which, admittedly, I showed little gratitude. The most interesting of these was with an unforgettable gentleman, C. W. Davis, who had been a high flyer in pre-war years but whose career had stalled at the rank of Executive Assistant, possibly through some misdemeanor in the dim and distant past. Mr Davis's job was to produce all the historic material for the guides on London Transport's day tours, which were then extremely popular, and though I must admit to finding visits to Westminster Abbey, Windsor Castle and such-like to check on the positioning of tombs and memorials quite enlightening, I felt my career was getting nowhere. What I did not then know was that, in the days before he was side-lined, Mr Davis had been deeply involved in the process of compulsorily acquiring independent country area operators at the time of London Transport's formation, and he must have possessed a font of personal knowledge of all those operators that I would love to have had access to when doing research on them many years later.

Spasmodic whingeing on my part about not having a 'proper' job led to me being offered a permanent post in the Staff Section of the Operating Manager's Department of Central Road Services dealing with various matters concerning personnel. After due consideration lasting all of half an hour, I turned the offer down on the basis that I had previously been involved with bus services and wanted to stay on that side of things. Perhaps naively, I regarded staff work as boring. Almost before I knew it, I was hauled up in front of our very big boss, the Chief Commercial & Public Relations Officer Mr D. McKenna (who, I believe, later made a name for himself on British Railways) to explain myself. Perhaps injudiciously, I told him that if I couldn't have a job within London Transport that interested me I might as well leave and work somewhere else for more money. Fortunately my bluff wasn't called, and about a week later I was told to report to Walworth bus garage to work on the Bus Running Control. For me, this was the turning point; I was about to become more deeply involved with bus operation at the raw end than I had ever dreamt possible as a mere class B clerk.

Bus Running Control was the name given to a squad of road officials whose task was to improve the regularity of operation on a range of bus routes badly affected by traffic congestion which was becoming an increasingly serious problem because of the rapid growth of car traffic throughout the central area of London. This was late 1955, before any of the major one-way schemes and other traffic improvement measures had been introduced, and delays could at times be horrendous. In a really bad rush hour it could take anything up to an hour to get from one end of Oxford Street to the other, and many other blackspots also had to be negotiated such as Tottenham Court Road, Park Lane, the Strand and Fleet Street. Outside the peaks and away from the central area, the opposite often applied and early running could be a problem. Originally started in a very small way as the Bus Running Squad back in 1951 to counter 'crawling' and to make drivers more 'time conscious', the emphasis had now changed and Bus Running Control was to be developed as a major force for service regularity.

From its little office at Walworth garage, the Bus Running Control's influence spread-eagled over many major bus routes all of which, except the 28 and 31, crossed central London. In charge, on the road, were two Chief Road Inspectors wearing plain clothes and *de rigeur* black homburg hats. Beneath them was a contingent of Road Inspectors (i.e. 'gold badge' inspectors) which eventually grew to 49, and some 150 ordinary 'silver badge' inspectors. However these were still early days in its development and, apart from Judy who did the filing and took a lot of phone calls, I was all that was provided in the way of administration. Luckily, as it grew bigger I got promotion and we took on more administrative staff. Our 'big boss' was J. H. Giffin, another long serving London busman whose main role was Divisional Superintendent of the South West Division located in the old tramway offices at Vauxhall to which we moved, lock stock and barrel, in due course. After being appointed Superintendent (Running) based at 55 Broadway, he arranged for Bus Running Control to join him there, so I found myself located back at head office just as the nineteen-fifties were drawing to a close.

Just occasionally in life you encounter someone who – unwittingly to themselves – exerts a disproportionately great influence on you, and for me James Giffin was one of these very rare people. Sharp and astute in a no-nonsense way, authoritarian but compassionate when the need arose, he had a remarkable ability to handle staff, to gain their confidence and earn their respect. I learnt a vast amount from him about man management, but when it came to learning about the nitty gritty of running buses, it was from the officials 'on the road' that I got my knowledge. These were the inspectors who manned what we called the 'periphery points' controlling the movement of some 32 bus routes, and the roving 'gold badge' inspectors who co-ordinated curtailments and other deviations from schedule in their endeavours to eliminate bunching and provide a reasonable semblance of service. The point inspectors produced graph-like reports which showed the day's operation at a glance, while their seniors were required to account for any failings to remedy major deficiencies in the service provision. We never attempted to deal with trolleybus services even when these ran parallel for long distances with bus services that we were controlling. By its very nature, the trolleybus did not lend itself to some of our practices, such as speeding late running recovery by getting vehicles on the same route to pass each other at stops, or by taking a vehicle out of a bunch and running it 'light' to a point further along the route where it could fill a gap. They also ran under a much more flexible regime and their inspectors were free to take a range of actions which long standing union agreements prevented bus officials from doing.

I quickly became totally immersed in my new job and soon got to know the strengths, weaknesses and foibles of everyone on the Bus Running Control as well as the problems that they faced. Frequent visits to the various periphery points to discuss public complaints or other day-to-day matters with inspectors meant that mine was much less mundane than any purely office based job, and I also passed many happy hours in J Lyons' tea shops chatting about bus matters and much more besides with gold badge inspectors, almost all of whom had a wealth of valuable experience behind them. Very soon I joined in the social activities too, helping to organise dinners and dances, arranging motor rallies, and fixing up visits to places of interest such as Wedgwood's Pottery and Vauxhall Motors.

Nowadays bus inspectors in London appear to be a thing of the past, but fifty years ago their presence was very high profile. On Bus Running Control each of our road officials was supplied with basic time lists of the services he was controlling, which were provided by the Schedules Office. These showed only the times at which the buses passed each official timing point during the working day, to which the officials added all the other things that they needed to know such as duty numbers, crews on spreadover shifts, journeys on which meal breaks were scheduled, short workings and various other pieces of information, often in hieroglyphics comprehensible only to themselves. Some officials were so versed at their job that they could remember the whole day's operating details without needing to refer to their time list other than very occasionally. The only items of technical equipment that the road officials had at their command were telephones, contact between themselves being maintained via a mixture of GPO telephones and internal ones which, in the main, were inherited from the tram and trolleybus network. The frustrations of trying to pass vital information down the line via the telephone system when it is having a bad day can be easily imagined.

The schedules themselves were often frustrating. These were compiled at 55 Broadway with minimum cost (or schedule efficiency, as it was called) as the main aim. Operability was never considered. Take route 22 (Putney Common to Homerton) as an example, which had a Monday to Friday allocation of 11 buses from Battersea garage and 20 from Hackney. The day's service from the western end would be scheduled to consist of a whole run of consecutive buses from Battersea whilst, likewise, Hackney buses started the service from the eastern end, and with few exceptions each garage's vehicles continued to follow each other around in blocks for the rest of the day. When it was time for meal reliefs to be provided, these would often be scheduled for each consecutive bus as it reached its crew changeover point. A schedule of this sort works very well when traffic is light and everything is running satisfactorily, but as soon as heavy delays start occurring in Sloane Street, Knightsbridge, Oxford Street, Cheapside and Bishopsgate, causing cumulative late running of perhaps 30 minutes or more, the operation falls apart.

The biggest problem for the road officials lay with the meal reliefs which, if they were not taken near enough to time, could produce repercussions throughout the day. Thus, on a bad day, the periphery inspector on route 22 at Great Eastern Street (Shoreditch) would be faced with a serious quandary. He had to provide a semblance of service to Homerton but could be faced with the arrival of a whole string of Battersea buses, all running very late, and all due for their meal reliefs when they got back to their changeover point at Chelsea. If they did not take their meal reliefs more or less on time, the operation of their next bus would be similarly late, extending disruption still further. He could curtail them at Shoreditch to get them back on time for their reliefs, but in doing so would decimate the service to Homerton. The periphery inspector at Sloane Street had the same problem with groups of Hackney buses travelling west. It was clear that, from an operational point of view, schedules could only really be workable at times of persistent late running if the two garage's buses were interspersed better and, where this was not possible, that at least the scheduling of consecutive meal reliefs could be avoided. On route 73 (worked by Tottenham and Mortlake garages) the situation was so bad that, each time a new schedule was sent down from Head Office, the route controllers concocted their own substantial variation on it with all sorts of pre-determined curtailments, projections and alterations to meal reliefs. A constant complaint from road officials was that schedule compilers, who sat in their office and presumably never got out much, clearly had no idea of the problems that their schedules caused. I suggested to Mr Giffin that we ought to try to do something about it, and taking route 22 as an example, I tentatively drew up a schedule incorporating the improvements that we needed. Within a few days I received a summons from the Schedules Superintendent asking me to see him to explain my logic for suggesting a switch to what, on paper at least, would almost certainly be more expensive scheduling.

The Schedules Superintendent was, by all accounts, not a man to be trifled with, especially by junior employees like me. Norman Eagles (for whom his staff had the nickname 'Fly', presumably because this is what eagles do) appeared, to outsiders, to run the huge, sprawling schedules office with a form of military precision. It was best not to be on the narrow circular staircase at the side entrance to 55 Broadway dead on 5pm when the compilers came rushing down like a torrent, having been released from their day's labours. Only much later did I learn from the *London Transport Magazine* that 'Fly' was a slightly eccentric timetable freak who had a substantial model railway network in his loft at home, which he and friends ran to strict timetables using clockwork trains. I duly reported to his office where, on the one and only occasion I ever met him, he turned out to be a very pleasant man who listened attentively to my tirade about problems 'on the road', asking numerous searching questions in return. The result was positive. A much improved new Monday to Friday schedule was compiled for route 22, but more importantly the principle was gradually established that schedules must be operationally realistic as well as cost efficient. Thereafter we enjoyed consultation with the schedules office on any new set of schedules proposed for our Bus Running Control services in order to eliminate, as far as was possible, any foreseeable operational difficulties contained within them.

Improved scheduling could only go so far in the provision of reliable bus services in the face of ever worsening traffic conditions. Shortening (or localisation) of cross-London routes offered a palliative for the future, but what we also needed was a much improved means of communication and control over day-to-day operations. Total reliance on telephone systems had severe drawbacks. Apart from technical problems which inevitably occurred from time to time, person-to-person communications could often prove fraught, especially when an inspector making a phone call to impart urgent information was unable to reach his colleague further down the road because the latter was away from the phone box dealing with a bus, or maybe a convoy of them. Calls to garages to obtain details of staff cuts (which got progressively worse as the decade wore on and peaked after the 1958 bus strike) and to pass on messages to crews could be especially frustrating as their lines were often engaged. New technology was badly needed to determine the whereabouts of each bus so that remedial action could be planned in advance and more accurately, and in our office on the third floor at 55 Broadway BESI (the Bus Electronic Scanning Indicator) was developed. A tentative suburban trial on a single scanner at Hanger Lane station, using a couple of RTLs from Shepherd's Bush garage on route 105, proved sufficiently encouraging for a full scale implementation of the early use of electronics on route 74, something that developed further in the following decade.

Below left Reliance by road officials on communication by telephone could produce a hit and miss result, but there was nothing else available to them at the time. Here, road inspector Grubb uses one of the internal network phones left over from the tramways and mounted on top of a former section box now emptied out but useful for storing overcoats etc. He refers to his time lists which, even though he has encased them in plastic, could be awkward to handle in wet or freezing weather or when winds were blowing a gale.
Ken Blacker collection

Below right Inspector Cook discusses something with the conductor of an RTW. If the bus is running late he may be authorising a curtailment or, if it is early, simply delaying it so that it does not depart more than two minutes ahead of time. Any instruction he gives must also be reported to the driver so that both members of the crew know what is needed.
Ken Blacker collection

Below GS 42 is seen on the stand at Rickmansworth. In May 1954 the 26-seater GS type replaced crew operated Ts on route 309 which ran from Rickmansworth to Harefield. The sliding windows, crash gearbox and sound of the Perkins engine made them look and sound rather like a provincial bus. They were however held in affection by both passengers and staff who at certain garages continued to refer to them as Cubs after the 20-seaters that they had replaced. GS 42 was destined, with GS 33, to be the last of the class in service on route 336A at Rickmansworth in March 1972. *Alan B Cross collection/LA*

Right By the time the short route 445 between Windsor and Datchet was converted to GS operation in July 1954 only one bus was required. In the past the route had seen such varied types as the C, STL, RT and RF and achieved some notoriety in 1946 when STL 2284 was allocated as part of the Pay-as you-Board experiment. In this view GS 35 is on the stand in a seemingly deserted St Albans Street adjacent to Windsor Castle. *Geoff Morant/LA*

Below Chelsham garage had GSs for three routes (464, 465 and 485) which interworked in a way that restrictive practices on Central Buses would not have permitted. The blind on GS 11 for a 464 short working and deviation via Pollards Oak is correctly set, even though the showing of parts of two labels may suggest otherwise. Such overlapping blind displays were a feature of Country Bus garages as a way of making the best use of material where many different permutations were needed, though they were rare on 'lazy' blind displays such as this one. Oxted station is where GS 11 is seen in the company of another member of the class in 1959. Garage journeys on the 464 from Oxted were of interest in that they ran in service on a 20-minute journey to CM with half of this run being along roads otherwise served only by Green Line. *Terry Russell/LA*

Above RT 62, upon being transferred to Hertford garage (HG) on 27th May 1955, became the only 2RT2 to see service at all five garages associated with operating the type in passenger service. The four central area garages were Chelverton Road (AF), Putney Bridge (F), Victoria (GM) and New Cross (NX) and it was while allocated to the last named that the vehicle was selected for further work. Following its two-year stay of execution in passenger service, RT 62 remained in the country area crossing the Thames to undertake learner duties at Addlestone garage (WY) from December 1957 to March 1958. Transferred in the same guise back to the central area the bus was allocated to a myriad of garages before its sale in November 1962; it was scrapped at Wrotham, Kent in February of the following year. *Alan Cross/ATB*

Right The reason seven 2RT2s were allocated to Hertford garage was the existence on route 327 of the Metropolitan Water Board's Bridge at Broxbourne, the weight limit imposed on the structure precluding the use of post-war RTs. Fortunately, the RTs of wartime manufacture were 15cwt lighter than their post-war counterparts for which they provided cover until rebuilding of the bridge was completed in 1957. This view at the country end of the 327 at Nazeing Common shows RT 93 before its run back to Hertford Bus Station. Initially blinds from the post-war STLs which the 2RT2s replaced saw further use, requiring a blanking strip being applied to the bottom of the via points display. Eventually, new blinds were produced although a side blind has been incorrectly fitted to RT 93. *Prince Marshall/ATB*

Bearing the highest bonnet number of the 2RT2s allocated to Hertford garage, RT 137 is recorded as having received its green livery on 26th May 1955; the vehicle being relicensed for service from 1st June. All of the 'magnificent seven' green 2RT2s were of the later chassis modification, encompassing 99 members of the class, that had resulted in their dynamos and air compressors becoming belt driven from the gearbox, an arrangement already adopted for the post-war model. All seven green 2RT2s were withdrawn from passenger service on 31st August 1957 and transferred to Potters Bar (PB). RT 137 soon found further duties as a staff bus and latterly a training vehicle at Reigate garage (RG) where it remained until finally withdrawn for disposal in February 1963. *Prince Marshall/ATB*

On 31st May 1955, RT 101 was withdrawn from passenger service while allocated to New Cross garage – the final day of 2RT2 operation in central London. It was not until January the following year that the bus was relicensed as a private trainer, ceasing to be required for the fulfilment of these duties in September 1959 and moving to Stockwell (SW) and ultimately Camberwell (Q) from where it was sold and subsequently scrapped. RT 101 was fitted during overhaul in September 1947 with 'high level' winding windows made by Hallam, Sleigh and Cheston; five other 2RT2s were similarly equipped. The result of the experiment was published in April 1954, which concluded that a retrospective introduction of this type of window to the existing fleet would be an uneconomic proposition. However, the design did become standard within the specification applied to the RF type and was put forward for consideration as an improvement in the construction of all future LT double deck vehicles. RT 101 is seen in the company of RTL 122 at London Bridge station. *Prince Marshall/ATB*

ROUTEMASTER
LONDON'S BUS OF THE FUTURE

RM 1, when it was unveiled in 1954, entered the scene at a time of diverging developments in the bus world, though trade commentators almost unanimously praised the Routemaster for its advances in bus design, echoing the reception given to RT 1 fifteen years earlier. Within two years it was to begin to look dated in the eyes of many. Indeed, the casual passer-by – unaware of the technical advances that were not visible on the surface – may well have wondered what was so special about 'London's Bus of the Future'. London Transport had carefully weighed up the merits of alternative layouts and had come to the conclusion that their new design was ideal for the capital; a view that its subsequent career was to strongly vindicate. Most bus enthusiasts who were around to see RM 1 when it was brand new speak of its bodywork design being a disappointment. The general feeling was that it was too boxy compared with the RT, and 'almost a hark back to the first batch of STLs' in Fred Ivey's view. David Ruddom remembers feeling squashed in at the front of the upper deck with the reduced leg room compared with RTs, though a plus point was that the plain front windows gave an uninterrupted view of the road and scenery ahead. RM 1 is seen in Vauxhall Bridge Road in the form in which it entered service. *Geoff Morant/JW*

Right After just a short time in service, RM 1 had to be taken off the road later in 1956 for a number of modifications, principally the installation of a conventional radiator in replacement of the underfloor one of the original design. A new engine of the latest AEC design was also fitted, as was power steering, a luxury almost unheard of on public service vehicles at the time, a 1951 Daimler double-deck design with it attracting little interest. Around the corner from the location of the previous view, the modified RM 1 turns left into the one-way system (as it was then laid out) at Grosvenor Place. *Prince Marshall/JW*

RM 2 – seen at a commercial vehicle gathering at AEC's Southall works in September 1958 – was at first intended for Green Line service out of Aldgate but ended up – after a short and unsuccessful period in the country area – on central bus service. In this view it is still carrying the country version of the Routemaster side poster that it was given while in service from Reigate garage. RML 3 and CRL 4 provided an opportunity to compare Leyland running units with the AEC units fitted to the first two prototypes, though London Transport – given free choice – would almost certainly have opted for a 100% AEC Routemaster fleet and had invited Leyland's participation at a fairly late stage of the new vehicle's design. RML 3 is seen at Marble Arch and CRL 4 was photographed at Hertford. *Capital Transport collection, Bruce Jenkins, Prince Marshall/JW*

Trips to Uxbridge

John A Gray

This feature is based on a set of slides taken by Peter Grace and a few others in the collection of Alan B Cross.

Uxbridge was to be reached by trolleybus, and was the gateway to countryside once across the River Colne bridge. Long before its closure to through motor traffic in 1976, the town's High Street bustled with busy public transport, reaching its maximum in the 1950s. The 607 trolleybus route had replaced the number 7 tram in 1936 to become one of London's most frequent trolleybus services. The all-Leyland F1 class vehicles, supplemented by K1s and, later, BUT Q1 class trolleys, ran up to a three-minute headway on weekdays and even at the same frequency on Sundays towards the end of the decade. Their swift acceleration from a standing start seems even now to be scarcely equalled by any contemporary diesel-engined bus, and their virtual silence when standing and mere gentle hum when moving are examples still to be attained by their successors. Seating 70 passengers, they could be a handful to conduct, particularly where large exchanges of passengers occurred at closely-spaced stops. Few people boarded at the Frays Bridge, Uxbridge, terminus except perhaps when the nearby Odeon cinema's evening programme ended. The first major boarding point was the High Street stop outside the Underground station. Claire, a conductress I knew, wouldn't even try to go round and take fares here. Instead, she'd remain stationed on the open platform to collect them, issuing tickets, as passengers alighted. Some regulars would deliberately tender a high value coin, say a florin (10p) for a three-half-penny fare in the expectation she would refuse it to avoid giving much coinage as change. She did not. The bus, and following alighting passengers, waited while she counted out coins and punched the right ticket. She had lightened her load of coins, and had less to count at the end of her shift. By then the next trolleybus had caught up, at once initiating a procession – since none could overtake – so familiar and frustrating.

Red RTs on the 204 to Hayes and 223 to Yiewsley and West Drayton came this way too, though not nearly so frequently, as did the 198 to Hayes and Hounslow from 1957. There were also four Green Line journeys an hour between routes 709, 710 and 711 worked by the ubiquitous RFs in succession to the 10T10s towards the end of 1951.

Meanwhile, red routes 222 and 224 (also its 224A/B offshoots in 1955/57), and Windsor garage's green country area routes 457/A/C, 458 and 459 turned right into Vine Street to collect the occasional passenger from outside the other railway station – the Western Region's still busy terminus named after the thoroughfare – on their ways through Cowley (the red routes and 458) or Iver Heath (457 group and 459).

In the other direction along the High Street from Belmont Road junction, the single-deck route 309 towards Harefield was replaced by RTs on the 347 in May 1953. High Wycombe garage's RT-worked route 455 towards Gerrards Cross came to be partly replaced by Amersham's RLHs on the 305 in May 1955. Finally, the South Midland coach journeyed its two-hourly way between Oxford and Victoria.

Throughout the 1950s, Uxbridge bus garage was situated on the north-eastern side of Oxford Road, Denham, thereby happening, by a few hundred yards, to be outside the central area whose buses it accommodated. No red bus route passed its twin double doors at the entrance to the straightforward building, which after nearly 30 years, was too small. In 1955, a second modest shed was erected alongside to ease the difficulty. These two buildings, together with Hounslow garage, coped with running Uxbridge's red routes through the decade and indeed until the present garage adjacent to the Underground station replaced it at the end of 1983.

The bus and coach forecourt at Uxbridge station sees RT 632 leaving for Windsor Castle fully laden with passengers, most of whom would have arrived here by Underground. The driver, seeing the Windsor Street traffic lights at red, will know it's safe to ease out gently in second gear in front of F1 class all-Leyland trolleybus 734. The passengers board the silent 20-year-old trolleybus from a 'Q' shelter, several of which adorned this station's vicinity and which were a common sight in the 1950s. The station forecourt was 'temporarily' equipped with overhead wiring in 1953 when, during the next spring and summer, delayed road works prevented access to the normal Frays Bridge terminating circle, hence the wires being routed from the Shepherd's Bush direction only. The RT's route information includes 'Upton Lea' for a route 457A working, at variance with the 'roofbox', but not with the above-platform display. 'Brazils' was a popular brand of sausages. *Peter Grace/JAG*

Here, the Underground station's High Street crescent forecourt plays host to the intended public transport and an interloping Ford car. A less-than-full RF 568 leaves on Saturday's largely hourly frequency route 459. The early version of blind includes the destination in full, necessitating the uncommon use of ultra-condensed capitals, hard to read at a distance, whereas the GS's abbreviated version shown opposite lost no meaning and was marginally easier on the eye. *Peter Grace/JAG*

When the time came in summer 1950 to reinstate a bus service to the outlying Riching's Park Estate south of Iver, Country Buses ran the duty in place of the previous route 220 cover, which had been withdrawn from there early in the war in 1939. The 459 went a different way to take in Iver Heath rather than Cowley, which was left to the red 222 and 224, the green 458 and to the Western Region's steam trains into Vine Street station. GS 78 looks as though it will take on a full load if all the queue boards. The bustle indicates it's a Saturday, judging by the number of working-age men in the picture, unemployment being at a low level in the later 1950s. Windsor provided the one bus needed for the route, which until autumn 1958 was a crew-operated RF. A GS then took over until the following spring, when an RF came back, now one-man operated. Both Leon & Co. Ltd the tobacconist's shop and Walton's the greengrocer were businesses located at many of London's Underground stations, and Uxbridge terminus – imbued with LT's pre-war architectural confidence and opened in December 1938 – was no exception. *Peter Grace/JAG*

Having turned right into Bakers Road, the driver accelerates RLH 4 in third gear past an RT at the 204 stop. The RLH's standard AEC engine produced a deeper, throbbing tone when compared with London's version as fitted to the RT. The blind had already been changed to show the next journey's destination of Beaconsfield (Saracen's Head). On introduction of the 305's extension from Gerrard's Cross to Uxbridge in 1955, the main road route 455 between the same outer points was reduced proportionately. The 305 had no need for a lowbridge bus, but the type had an official allocation alongside RTs – not, perhaps, the conductor's preference. *Alan B Cross collection/JAG.*

Upper right Distinctive but hardly handsome, Weymann-bodied 14T12 sub-type T 746 stands in front of another at some distance from the kerb by stop No. 3. In a driving test, the driver – perhaps the one strolling with his conductress towards the photographer – would not have passed in view of his failure to stop the bus close enough. These melodious buses were replaced at Uxbridge garage on the 224 group of routes by the slightly newer Leyland TDs towards the end of 1958. On a point of detail, several of these Ts were seen to have a green, Country Bus style, triangular badge at the head of their AEC radiators, unlike T 746 here with the correct Central Bus blue and red version. The white rectangle above the first nearside window contains no route number stencil, by now fallen into disuse. *Alan B Cross collection/JAG*

Right Regarded by many as better proportioned than their Weymann-bodied peers, the Mann Egerton versions of T and TD sub-types were useful intermediates till the easier to drive RFs came on stream in the early fifties. A saying 'If it looks right, it is right' suits this design apart from, perhaps, a slightly aggressive look imparted by the radiator and wings cut to clear the dumbirons. A streaky sunlit reflection from a white Mk2 Ford Consul heading towards the Market Hall rather spoils the clean offside line of TD 128. The driver has chosen to leave his cab's sliding door in the open position, replicating the draughty ventilation of earlier motor buses with London's standard doorless cabs. *Peter Grace/JAG*

Turning from Belmont Road into Bakers Road, RT 2547 is shortly to arrive at the wide side entrance to the Underground station, having come from Ruislip on the weekdays section of the 223. The bus is clean and well presented with service information accurately displayed, complete with newly fitted left trafficator obligingly operating as the bus passes the head of a line of parked cars, a Morris saloon from the early nineteen-thirties equipped with the popular coolant thermometer atop its radiator cap. By now in the late fifties, parking is cluttering the streets. *Peter Grace/JAG*

Well before high rise building denied Bakers Road much sunshine, this lively weekend scene at the open end of the cul-de-sac includes three buses leaving and three more driving in to their stops or standing at them. Leading the outward bound into the short stretch of Belmont Road to reach High Street is RT 295, continuing to carry the original style of bodywork. This central bus has been lent to the country's High Wycombe garage to help shift the surge in passengers, many of whom may visit Beaconsfield (mentioned on the slip board at the foot of the lower deck front window) with its popular Bekonscot model village. Route information is provided only briefly by a paper bill in the front route aperture and nowhere else in view. Next in line is a green RF on country route 458 to Slough, but whose garage journeys continue beyond to Windsor. Facing the opposite way, Windsor's RF 577 on the 458 is sandwiched between two more red RTs. *Peter Grace/JAG*

A squatting figure in the passenger shelter at bus stop No. 5 in Bakers Road is content to ignore green RT 4555, whose body was removed from SRT 158 in September 1954, and the passing RT 820, while a third RT comes in from Belmont Road, behind. The rear of Weymann-bodied T 757 of the 14T12 sub-type stands opposite at stop No. 4, displaying a descriptive blind for a short 224 working to Harmondsworth. Garston garage's RT 4555 shows blinds with white lettering on blue ground which were intended to lend emphasis to 'express' routes additional to the word itself. The highly numbered route was a mid-1950s' effort to stimulate and cater for longer distance traffic between Uxbridge and Welwyn Garden City via Watford, St Albans and Hatfield new town without going to the extent of providing a full-blown Green Line service. The conductor has set the route points blind to show the short Rickmansworth to St Albans working. Welwyn Garden City was one of three distant places a passenger could travel by bus from Uxbridge without changing, an 85-minute journey. Hemel Hempstead by 347 and Harpenden by 321/351 took slightly longer. *Alan B Cross/JAG*

The 1958 Bus Strike

Ken Tuddenham

When I started with London Transport in 1955, there were murmurings that the pay was not keeping up with that of other jobs and this led to a high level turnover of staff, not only at Fulwell depot, where I worked, but throughout the network. The pay was okay but was only good if some extra work was done – overtime or rest day working. The Transport and General Workers Union were forever pushing our case for better pay, and at the end of 1957 they really raised their game. Eventually, they decided that there was no other option but to strike. Each depot and garage was a branch of the union which meant that the members at each location had the opportunity to vote on the issue; ninety-nine per cent of our staff voted for a strike, believing that it wouldn't last very long – nobody thought that it would go on for as long as it did. Despite various efforts by a number of official bodies to avoid it, the strike was set to start on Monday 5th May 1958.

On Sunday 4th May, everything ran as normal, but the public had been beefed up by the press that an all-out strike would start the following day. There wasn't any hostility towards us and in general they were sympathetic to our cause. The trolleybuses ran in that night, and after cleaning they all had their poles pulled down and their electrics switched off. The only concession made that night was for the staff trolleybus to take crews home; this duty just did its first half. This was two trips to Kingston and Twickenham, with the crew just getting paid for the short time that they were at work. Once it got into the depot, all the big green doors were pulled to; it looked really strange seeing them fully closed – this was the only time I saw this. The maintenance staff had a hard job closing the doors as it had been a long time since they had last done this.

Half of the staff thought that the strike would be over quickly, while the other half thought that it would take a long time to resolve – mainly conductors. After about three weeks, many staff started to get uptight about the situation; some were buying their houses at this time and started looking for other jobs as they had bills to pay. A few found temporary work gardening, but for most of the time we were just twiddling our thumbs. On a personal level, the main problem was boredom, but I used to help my dad on his allotment to relieve that. Strangely, very few people left the depot at this time; as I recall, two went on the railway and three got jobs at London Airport as it was then called.

The catering staff were not on strike, and the Chief Depot Inspector allowed us to go into the canteen for a cup of tea. Here we discussed the strike but were not allowed to have any union meetings – these were held in 'The Jolly Blacksmith' pub which was at Sixth Cross Road, a short distance from the depot. At Hounslow and Twickenham bus garages, the staff would not even go to the canteen. There had always been rivalry between trolleybus and motorbus staff when they were working on the same section of road. Now it became heated as the Central Bus staff didn't even like us going onto the Board's premises. Some days, a few of the Isleworth and Hanwell lads came over to be with us and we also went to their depots – this was because we were all former London United Tramways depots and considered ourselves one body.

Friends and other people I knew, who were used to travelling on public transport, used cycles or just had to walk to their place of work. It has to be borne in mind that at the time not many people owned cars, so unless people worked locally they had to arrange for a lift to get in. There were certain elements of the public who swore at us but on the whole there was no resentment.

The maintenance staff and overhead crews were not involved with the dispute and came in for work as normal. However, as the trolleybuses could not be moved easily, there was very little they could do apart from cleaning and some routine maintenance – the only

A blot on the landscape of the nineteen-fifties was the bitter bus strike in May and June of 1958 and the factors that led up to it. Since the end of the second world war, London busmen's pay had fallen behind that of other jobs that would attract men who might otherwise apply for work on the buses. London Transport had used two tactics to relieve the staff shortage that resulted: the employment of women as conductors from 1950 (women were employed in this role during the war but were laid off afterwards) and, from 1956, bringing men over from the West Indies and Ireland (even setting up temporary hostels to accommodate those taken on). Neither tactic was looked upon approvingly by the Trade Union, who saw each as a way around paying staff a better wage, and nor did such measures solve the problem. In 1955 there was a 7.5% shortage in the number of drivers and conductors needed to run the services and this shortage had doubled for a brief period five years later despite there being fewer services to run following the cuts that resulted from the strike. The work that they could perform was to move a few of the vehicles out of the depot into the maintenance area. The 'running shift' – those who went out to breakdowns, substituted trolleybuses when necessary, sometimes allocated vehicles for service and did a bit of shunting – were on 'fire-watching' duties (now known as security). The general hands did little else than keep the depot tidy. The overhead staff were also not participating in the strike, and they did go out to check the overhead from time to time. As May dawned, London Transport was aware that they were in for a long haul and brought into the Works a lot of trolleybuses ahead of schedule. This allowed the work to be got on with and meant that there wouldn't be too big a backlog when the dispute was over. Of course the Works could only take so many vehicles and by Tuesday 13th May the staff had completed everything they were supposed to do and became victims of a 'lock-out'. However, to avoid any confrontation, they were told to go home and would get full pay.

The Works staff were normally brought in by staff buses from various parts of London; these vehicles were kept at various garages, but with the start of the strike they were entombed so could not get out and over to Fulwell. The works staff had to make their own way over and did this by giving and getting lifts, or travelling on the suburban railway to Fulwell station. The same situation occurred at Aldenham and Charlton Works – vehicles were brought in early for overhaul and when the staff ran out of work they also were sent home on full pay.

London Transport was hoping, right up until the last minute, that the strike would be avoided. They were in the business of running buses and, at the time of a high staff shortage, needed to keep the recruitment momentum maintained. Therefore they were taking on staff almost until strike day. They had started working for London Transport, but new staff didn't join the TGWU until they went to their depots or garages. London Transport couldn't terminate their employment as they wouldn't come back when the strike was over. The conductors were kept at Chiswick Works and had classroom and some on-bus instruction using RT training buses running around the premises; new drivers acted as members of the public for them. Obviously there was no recruitment during the strike period and those who had been taken on had an easy seven weeks doing nothing much else than drink cups of tea in the Chiswick canteen. Afterwards, there would have been new staff going to garages and depots all over the fleet but, as it turned out, there was only one conductor coming to Fulwell – when he eventually arrived, he was a 'know-it-all' who was soon put in his place! At the time, we had three conductors who were driver-training at Fulwell; as they were members of the union they obviously didn't work. When they restarted their training they had to go over to Colindale to finish it off. One of our trolleybus drivers was at Chiswick at the time, training for his PSV badge – this would allow him to drive motorbuses on staff private hires. He had to pack it in when the strike started and go back and finish it off at London Transport's convenience. I availed myself of this facility and obtained my PSV badge in 1960, two years ahead of the rest of the drivers in the depot.

The strike was all about giving the Country Bus staff the same level of pay increase the Central Bus staff were asking for. We were all solid on this and not a single bus or trolleybus ran during the dispute. Eventually, LT and the TGWU came to some sort of agreement, but the strike had achieved nothing and we got paid no more than we were originally offered. On 20th June, word soon got round that the strike had been called off and that day the depot was opened up and we went in to find out the duty we would be on the following day – we picked up the duty that we would have worked had the strike not taken place. Once the engineers knew that the strike had been called off, they went out into the depot straight away and placed the trolley poles of all the vehicles on the overhead wires; this was to charge up the batteries and build up the air pressure. They then got the trolleybuses prepared for service the next day when everything ran out as normal.

There was one fact that affected trolleybus staff and not motorbus staff and that was that drivers were concerned about muck that had accumulated on the running wires

degree to which overtime by the operating staff disguised the staff shortage was brought into the open in August and September 1954 by an unofficial ban on overtime and rest day working which made it necessary for London Transport to introduce emergency schedules. The availability of overtime was viewed by some staff as a useful way of earning a higher than standard hourly rate for their efforts and by others with some degree of resentment that it was a necessary part of their earnings in order to make ends meet. The pay claim that was to lead to the 1958 bus strike was first lodged in October 1957. Following a series of failed negotiations, their claim went to arbitration the following February. The award that resulted offered an increase of about one-third of the amount of the Union's claim to Central Bus staff and none at all to Country Bus staff. The Union refused to accept it. On 29th April, the Union gave one week's notice of its intention call out all London bus and trolleybus drivers and conductors in the central and country areas. The strike, from 5th May, was 100% solid and continued for almost seven weeks until being called off without the busmen's demands being met. John Gent, who worked at London Transport's headquarters, recalls: "Our office was selected as a Control Centre, not that there was much to control! It was manned for 24 hours while the strike was on so I spent several nights sleeping on a camp bed at 55 Broadway. We had to record details of any buses operated by the People's League for the Defence of Freedom or any unusual happenings. Once the strike was over we had to record loadings on a number of routes which were on a list for possible withdrawal and there is no doubt a lot of traffic was lost because of the strike." There was ill feeling between the staff and management for years to come. *Capital Transport collection/JW*

during the dispute. Not only were we anxious about the general state of the overhead, but we were also worried about the filth, and any litter that the wind had blown into the troughing under bridges. We were told that a couple of trolleybuses had been cleaning out the wires on the preceding night (Thursday 19th June) – presumably London Transport were sensing an ending of the strike and gave instructions for some wire cleaning, maybe at all depots. We were informed that the maintenance staff had cleaned Twickenham, Teddington and in the Kingston vicinity but hadn't done the extremities of our district – Hammersmith and Wimbledon, so we asked for iron skids to be fitted to the first trolleybuses on each route so that the overhead would be clean. The maintenance staff refused on the basis that they only fitted them in frosty weather and considered that 21st June did not fall into that category. It has been brought to my attention that enthusiast Tony Belton, when he was doing his paper round at about 8am on Sunday 15th June, saw Finchley's 932 travelling south along Holloway Road – it was near Holloway bus garage. The fact that these trips were being carried out when few potential passengers would have been around would have allayed stories that the strike was over.

The trolleybuses went straight back into service with the same carbons in the trolley heads that they had run in with almost seven weeks previously. Even though there had been minimal cleaning, it should be borne in mind that it was summertime so there was little flashing and arcing from dirty overhead; even the Brentford Half Acre loop didn't take too long to become polished as the 655s and 657s turned there as well as our 667s. The power had been kept on during the strike as London Transport was concerned about overhead being stolen. A notice was placed on the depot forecourt stating 'Power is on'. This drew the fact to the staff's attention but also acted as a deterrent to metal thieves.

I hadn't driven a trolleybus for several weeks and when I first got in the cab of one, everything seemed a bit strange; as an example, I'd forgotten the order of the positions of the switches that controlled the lights and windscreen wipers. After a couple of minutes in the depot yard I became used to everything again. Everybody was glad to get back to work and bearing in mind that we'd all lost a lot of money during the dispute, most drivers and conductors did a lot of overtime and rest day working to make up for it. The management made the most of this and were able to cover all of the duties for many weeks afterwards. The strike had done a lot of damage and many service cuts followed as people had found other means of moving around – many had bought motorbikes or cars, probably through hire purchase schemes. Pay continued to be an issue for many years.

Right By 1958, wartime utility bus bodies were becoming quite rare in Britain (the last had run in London in 1953), both because of their austere specification and, very often, deterioration of the poor-quality wood from which the framing of many had been made. There is no sign of this on these two vehicles that were operated by the People's League for the Defence of Freedom. CRX 540 in Grosvenor Place has a Strachan utility body mounted on a Bristol K6A chassis and appears to have received a recent repaint for independent R Taylor & Son, having been new to Thames Valley. FTD 618, a 15-year-old Daimler CWA6 with Duple body from the Lytham St Annes Corporation fleet, is seen at East Croydon station. It retains the original single opening window per side on each deck. Duple bodied a high proportion of the wartime CWA6 buses and their bodies tended to last quite well despite the slender-looking pillars. The shell-back rear dome characteristic of Duple's interpretation of the utility specification is evident in this view. The People's League for the Defence of Freedom was a far right political organisation that had recently been set up by a former Liberal parliamentary candidate. It began a free bus service between Waterloo and Bank by buying a former Tynemouth Weymann bodied Regent of late 1930s vintage. Further routes very soon followed and about another 20 buses. These came from a south London dealer, though it has never been clear whether they were bought, hired or loaned by someone sympathetic to the League's aims. At first, passengers were carried free of charge, but two weeks after services began on 31st May, London Transport gave permission for a 6d flat fare to be taken; by now there were seven routes over some of the busiest traffic corridors. In addition a small number of commercial operators were granted licences for a total of seven routes in the suburbs and the country area. The services continued running until strike was called off on 20th June, London Transport's services restarting the following day. The People's League continued in existence and went on to run a parcels service during a three-week 'work to rule' of postal workers in January 1962. *Alan B Cross collection, Prince Marshall/AT*

Seen in the Wandsworth car park where the League's vehicles were kept, DBC 221 and 224 were ex-Leicester Corporation AEC Renown 64-seat six-wheelers from the final batch of 16 of that model to be built, in 1940. They were on the long-wheelbase 664-series chassis, of which the largest fleet had been the LGOC's LT-class single-deckers of 1931 best known as the 'scooters'. Leicester had received an earlier batch of nine Renown double-deckers in 1939 which had Northern Counties bodies of that firm's very rounded style of the time – one survives as a preserved vehicle. Although the body order for the 1940 buses went to Metro-Cammell they closely resembled the Northern Counties bodies, the giveaway evident in this view being the style of cab front, of a characteristic less bulbous Metro-Cammell style. They had AEC 7.7-litre oil engines and preselective gearboxes but the six-wheel chassis and greater weight made them much less nimble than the similarly-powered standard London STL buses of 1935–39, all by then withdrawn. So far as can be judged from photos, the vehicles used by the League seem to have been in quite good structural condition despite by then being quite (sometimes very) old by the standards of most major operators. Even then they formed an interesting collection, several having links to earlier episodes of bus history. *Alan B Cross collection/AT*

Above right BTC 624 was a 1936 Leyland Lion LT7c with standard Leyland 34-seat body and is seen in Streatham. The header tank alongside the bonnet suggests that it still had the so-called 'Gearless' torque converter transmission, useful in the heavy traffic seen here. Alongside is Southdown 24 (TUF 24) a Beadle-Commer TS3 new in 1957. The contrast between the low-pitched rumble from the Lion's four-cylinder oil engine and the snarl from the Commer's TS3 two-stroke engine (built in the Tilling-Stevens works in Maidstone) would have been as striking as the visual comparison. *Alan B Cross collection/AT*

Right Lancaster Corporation simply accepted whatever registration number was issued and also showed it as the fleet number in the early post-war years, as was still evident when HTC 615, a 1947 Crossley SD42/3 with standard Crossley body, was running for the PDLF. Crossley had become quite a popular choice among municipal bus fleets in the early post-war years, more usually for double-deckers and partly because of the rapid delivery that could usually be offered, but then faded from favour. The bus is parked at Wandsworth opposite some wartime prefabs.
Alan B Cross collection/AT

At first glance, BFN 934, a Leyland Titan TD7 seen in Park Lane, might easily be mistaken for a wartime utility bus because of its angular outline. In fact, it was built in 1940 for the East Kent Road Car Co Ltd, then having a lowbridge body built to that operator's standard pre-war style by Park Royal. Although vehicle designs had yet to be affected by the war, there had been a sharp change in vehicle needs away from the south-east coastal areas to where buses were needed more urgently and this bus was one of ten diverted to Crosville Motor Services Ltd. However, in 1952 all received new highbridge bodies built in Crosville's own workshops to what by then seemed a very austere-looking design. Unusually they retained the 53-seat capacity they had with the original bodies rather than the 56 more usual with the full-height layout. *Prince Marshall/AT*

DUC 904 had roots linking it to the days when independent bus operators ran scheduled services in central London. One of the biggest had been the City Motor Omnibus Co Ltd, with strong ties both to Leyland and the use of six-wheel buses. After its business was acquired by the LPTB in 1934, it was not surprising that the same applied to the City Coach Co Ltd, run by much the same management team but based in Brentwood, though with a mainly single-deck fleet. This Leyland Tiger TS7D – the 'D' signifying that both axles in the rear bogie were driven – dated from 1937 and had Beadle bodywork seating 43 passengers, at the time the highest capacity in a front-engined single-decker operating in Britain. There had been 36 buses of this form in the City Coach fleet, the earlier ones of 1935-6 on the TS7T chassis; similar but with trailing rearmost axle. *Jack Law/AT*

Reigate Remembered

Derek Fisk

Arriving at Reigate office in May 1950, at the end of two years of National Service seemed like a dream coming true. I had started in London Transport at the end of 1946 as a Junior Clerk in the Staff department, despite having expressed an interest in bus service planning. As it turned out, this was a fortunate beginning, because within this central department I gained a useful overview of the whole organisation. It had also helped me to appreciate that Country Bus and Coach operations were far more diverse than those of Central Buses, so this helped to focus my ambition.

I was very lucky to be accepted at Reigate as there were no vacancies then in the operating headquarters; indeed, I was to become the first new male member of the office staff there since the end of the war! Someone persuaded them to take me on as a supernumerary, and what a fortunate posting this was for me. For almost a year I was, in effect, the holiday and sickness cover in the different sections – stops, stands, route approvals, tours and excursions, public letters, etc, – and thus served a valuable apprenticeship. I have often said that I learnt my trade at Reigate.

London Transport's whole management organisation was on strictly functional lines with separate departments being responsible for operations, mechanical engineering, civil engineering, supplies, finance, staff (including industrial relations policy), legal, publicity, etc. Within each department there was a strict hierarchy of grading of each individual job from the top management down to the humblest clerk. Every vacancy that arose was advertised at the appropriate level across the whole organisation so that, apart from those posts or functions for which specialist qualifications or experience were required, it was theoretically open to each member of staff to apply for any vacancy at the next grade of management, without necessarily following a straight upward progression in one particular area of expertise.

The office building at Reigate was an imposing three floor structure between the original East Surrey garage in Bell Street and the new large garage in Lesbourne Road from which it was originally intended to maintain the whole of the General Country Services fleet of buses and Green Line coaches. This had been watered down in 1935 when Chiswick took over the green as well as the red fleet, but Reigate still managed some independence. A footpath ran diagonally between the office and garage buildings, leading towards the main Reigate–Redhill road, and a rather convenient orchard just behind the office into which, in the autumn, some careful scrumping expeditions could be mounted.

Apart from a small office for the District Superintendent (South), the local operating official, the ground floor was occupied by the schedules office which, though part of the whole Schedules department, had a much closer relationship with the traffic section upstairs than their Central Bus colleagues had at 55 Broadway. Apart from vehicle and duty schedule compilation, this office also drew up the wording for the destination blinds on the buses, and was going through a particularly busy period with the restoration of full blind displays after the austere minimal wartime blinds. On the top floor were the typing pool, performing all typing work for the whole building, and the Traffic Audit office, a revenue control section maintaining all financial records of fares collected and tickets issued.

Senior management and the operating department occupied the middle floor. Here were the staff section, one for service planning (Traffic Investigation), another dealing with the operations functions already mentioned, a training unit and a 'general' section tackling all the other little jobs which sat less easily elsewhere.

At that time within LT generally, automatic entitlement to sick pay was normally available only to salaried staff, but a unique feature in the Country department was that all staff at every level did receive sick pay through compulsory membership of the Country Bus Friendly Society. This fund had been set up by East Surrey in 1918 with equal contributions being received from the staff and from management, the whole operation being managed by the fund secretary whose office was also on this first floor.

Those early months at Reigate were an education in other ways. For example, Country Buses ran bus or coach excursions from almost every garage to the Derby at Epsom Races, parking them at Tattenham Corner on a patch of ground that was large enough to take all those vehicles and still offer spare room for private car parking. Reigate Office staff had the 'privilege' of running that car park, taking the cash and showing visitors to their places. We were taken up to the Downs in an old bus, which we used as our base. I took part and distinguished myself that first year by taking someone's money from them without realising that the last space had been filled, being later confronted by the rather angry driver, accompanied by my boss and a policeman, demanding redress after he had finally fetched up in a different car park where he had had to pay again.

Office hours were 9 to 5 and strictly observed. Up to a middle level of management everyone had to sign in the daily attendance book, across which a red line was drawn by one of the staff clerks at 9.05am. If you were late you were summoned to the section head to explain yourself. Most of the office people lived in and around Reigate, so had little problem in this respect but others like myself came from further away and one young lady was from East Grinstead. For me, a convenient 406 was due in the town about 8.50am. However two steam trains were scheduled over Reigate station level crossing at 8.45am and, if either was slightly late, getting in on time became a nail-biting exercise. If we were lucky, a friendly crew on a garage journey might pick us up at the Town Hall; thus honour would be satisfied – just.

At the other end of the day it happened that both a 411 towards Redhill and a 424 to East Grinstead were due at the nearby stops just on the hour. Again, those involved might just be lucky enough to avoid a 15 or 30 minute wait for the next bus. This office adherence to strict timekeeping also applied at lunch time. This was not a problem if you ate in the garage canteen, but more so if one chose to use a café in the town. There was one in West Street which did excellent puddings but, if you had lunched with one of the girls from the office and chose to dawdle back through the park, you could each jeopardise your time-keeping record. The other little rule worth mentioning is that, if you were staying on for booked overtime, you had to have a half-hour break before starting. The canteen did well from orders for 'double beans on toast' on such occasions. One evening I had finished overtime after 8.30pm and was walking into the town to get the 9 o'clock 406 home, when I was stopped by a policeman who wanted to know what a young fellow like me was doing abroad in the town at that time of night!

There was also one other regular excursion from the office as Reigate's office staff were paid four-weekly by cheque cashed at the Reigate branch of Westminster Bank. We were each allowed 20 minutes, taking it in turns to go down to that bank in the High Street to cash our cheques. By no means everyone in those days had bank accounts, and it was some while before salaries were credited direct to one's account. (Staff at 55 Broadway had a similar facility within the building, collecting their money from the Paying Cashier's office.)

A pleasantly sociable atmosphere prevailed at Reigate office, and some light hearted fun broke the surface from time to time. All the typing was carried out in the pool and, while some of the girls were qualified in shorthand, taking dictation from the senior people, the rest of us submitted work either in longhand or, more normally, by recording on Dictaphone machines. With these, one spoke through a trumpet mouthpiece on to a rotating wax cylinder which the typist played back to produce typed work, afterwards shaving a layer off the cylinder for re-use. The mouthpiece was detachable and sound magnification could be compromised by stuffing scrap paper into it or, one occasion, a piece of fish. The gentleman concerned was puzzled by the typist's inability to hear his words until, in time, the fish began to smell. At a time of continued food rationing we were berated more for wasting food than office efficiency!

The annual dinner, held in the local Drill Hall, was always well attended, and A. H. Hawkins himself would come, though his choice of after dinner jokes wasn't always suitable for mixed company. Office tea and coffee, and buns or biscuits, were brought round by the garage canteen staff twice a day, making a welcome break, but it wasn't unknown in the interval before they returned to collect the empties for someone to call "catch" and to look up to see a cup flying in your direction. You always caught it. You had to!

All this was only a background to the imperative of planning and running an appropriate bus and coach service for our passengers at a time when, although fuel rationing had ended, demand for our services was still pretty buoyant, boosted by the new London overspill housing estates being built and with planning of the six New Towns getting under way. That buoyancy in peak hours, evenings and weekend demand contrasted with slack trade during midweek off-peak hours, except on local market days. With fridges or freezers still being a relative luxury, food shopping was a daily activity, but not usually by bus, as there were good local shops within easy walking distance. Trips to the cinema were a frequent evening outing, as were weekend journeys for pleasant days out. The response to this latter called for several buses being needed for Green Line duplication.

I was lucky in getting two quick moves up the promotion ladder in 1951, first into a post in the Operating section, followed shortly afterwards by my applying to fill a vacancy in the Traffic Investigation section, in which all the service planning was done. This was what I was really interested in doing, and in preparation for this I had been using my free time profitably to gain as much geographical knowledge of our extensive area up to 30 miles radius from London. As some of the routes, especially in the northern parts, were not regular or even daily services, this called for some ingenuity in itinerary planning. I once alighted from a 384 at Tonwell to walk across the fields to Chapmore End, served by the occasional Cub on the 333 from Hertford. My boarding with a staff pass at this remote terminus surprised the driver who, asking from where I had come, corrected my phonetic pronunciation by saying *"Tunnel,* my boy".

Although not selected for the post then I found to my surprise three months later – when the successful candidate was suddenly transferred to Chiswick to be Personal Assistant to the CME – that I had been the second choice and got my deeply desired promotion. This incident illustrated two exceptions to standard rules, firstly that PA posts were filled outside the normal procedures, and secondly that if a vacancy recurred within a few months, and there was a suitable second choice, the job was a not re-advertised.

Working on service planning at a time of much change really was the dream coming true. Stimuli for change included the need to serve new developments, to increase capacity on inadequate schedules, to apply faster running times using the RT's superior acceleration, or the annual seasonal changes for pleasure resorts like Windsor or the Surrey Hills. Single deck rejuvenation came rather later so, until late 1953, the 20-seat Cubs remained heavily engaged on a wide variety of routes, ranging from the busy, frequent 333 to Bengeo, or 464/5 based on Oxted, to market day only services like 329A from Datchworth to Hitchin. I rode that one Saturday afternoon standing in the doorwell because the driver could hardly afford to leave passengers behind on such an infrequent route. Even the 464 had two schooldays only journeys to Staffhurst Wood school, a place not otherwise on the bus map. When, from late 1953, the 26-seat GS type started to replace the Cubs, some were also used instead of lightly used large saloons on routes like 389 and 445. Thus began the expansion of one-man operation followed a little later by the first conversions of RFs to OMO. Initially, these converted buses had a wider cab for mounting the ticket machine (later discontinued) and the official photograph shows a lady passenger, who was in fact a member of the Reigate office team, buying a ticket.

Inadequacy was principally a morning peak problem because of the conflict between factory/office travel and children going to school. During the war, concentrated demands like this had led to schemes for local staggering of working hours to spread demand over a longer period. Compromises were negotiated through a network of wartime industry/transport operator liaison groups, which continued for some decades afterwards, achieving some notable successes in places like Stevenage and Crawley, for example. A different scenario arose from our inheritance of Grays area Eastern National routes. These included an economical working whereby the same buses first took workers to Bata at East Tilbury then continued on to the oil refineries at Shellhaven and Coryton. Fine. And then Bata announced it was adopting a shorter working week whereby its hours would conflict directly with those of the refineries, thus doubling the number of buses and crews needed to serve these people. I had to accompany the Divisional Superintendent to a meeting with these establishments, where we managed to get agreement that Bata would shorten its total hours by giving its staff a half day off on Friday, leaving the existing hours unchanged on other days. A few extra early off-peak Friday afternoon trips to Bata were a far cheaper and easier option for us.

By far the biggest planning job for the Traffic section was the long running series of negotiations with each of the New Town Development Corporations on the geography and construction phasing of each town and on how we would provide adequate bus services. Each corporation had its own ideas, of course, and while some understood the need for good penetration of the estates, Harlow's approach was to confine buses to the spine roads. Despite our arguments we eventually had to conform but, in later London Transport life I found myself at regular meetings with the locally elected town Council (which had succeeded the Development Corporation) disgruntled about the resultant lack of penetration of estates by local bus services. As those estate roads were not engineered to accept buses the situation was one which neither of us could change.

One interesting interlude occurred in those early Reigate years. The garage, having much spare space, was selected as the storage point for preserved road vehicles. These were lined up along the north-west wall, and were incongruously joined by trams 290 and 1025. These had arrived mounted on low loaders but, thus mounted, were too tall for the garage entrance. They were each dismounted on the forecourt, which was on a downward slope, and then had carefully to be winched down on their own wheels to their allotted parking spaces, manoeuvres which several of us watched with interest. I'm not sure whether the rigid 290 was easier to guide than the bogie car, but each was safely parked to await, some years later, their transfer to Clapham.

The four and a half years I spent in the Traffic section at Reigate were personally highly satisfying, and I hope that I was able to contribute a constructive approach to bus service planning from what I learnt there, even if as time went on we were feeling the effects of the mood swing of the travel market away from public towards private transport. To be fair, I wanted to be part of that too, having married and moved to Norbiton (still on the 406 to work) and was learning to drive a car, helped greatly by a colleague who lived in Surbiton and who used a 20 year old Ford for his work journey. He both let me practise on the homeward journey and also let me take the driving test in it.

I borrowed the same car only a few days later when, having gained a promotion to become Chief Clerk at the newly established North Divisional office, based at Garston, my wife and I were able to move to Hemel Hempstead with the luxury of private transport. That post had arisen as a result of a fundamental change of thinking within the Country Bus organisation, and the start of a gradual erosion of the top-down approach to management which had characterised London Transport since its earliest days. B. H. Harbour, who had been the Operating Manager at Reigate since the retirement of East Surrey's founder A. H. Hawkins in 1946, was appointed an LTE board member and succeeded by Geoffrey Fernyhough, hitherto the North Divisional Superintendent, who wanted to devolve more day-by-day responsibility to local management. Hence the new enlarged

North and South Divisional organisations, whose offices were to comprise a Superintendent and his Deputy, a chief clerk, and three two-man sections dealing with staff, operations and traffic matters respectively.

We were thus much closer to the daily operations than at Reigate, and this kept me directly connected with the growth of the five northern New Towns with whose initial planning I had been earlier familiar. It was also a time of a number of anxieties in running bus services, even if there were also some exciting developments taking place as well. One innovation was Express route 803 from Uxbridge via Watford and St Albans to Welwyn Garden City, using standard RTs, but at significantly quicker timings than normal stopping services. That these timings were, to say the least, adventurous became apparent fairly early on when some drivers struggled to avoid late running. Normally, running time was determined by joint road testing between operating officials and a union representative but, in this case, the Divisional Mechanical Inspector had exercised his considerable skills in determining the schedule. He, by the way, was a keen fisherman who once claimed that he never read fiction, yet came into the office one day reading a fishing journal! Some observations of timekeeping were called for and I, together with other divisional staff, were employed on riding-on-bus tests. Standing on an RT platform at high speed is quite hair raising but, despite co-operative crews, it was obvious that some easing of a tight schedule was needed. Even so, it had been enjoyable to be out and about in service instead of just forming opinions in an office.

I mentioned anxiety. This period was one of difficulty in retaining staff on awkward shift work faced with competition with straight shift employers like Vauxhalls at Luton, for example. Trouble was that demands for such work were variable and sometimes our former employees would find themselves laid off and wanting to return. Yet at the same time we were recruiting from further away, and even going to the lengths of setting up hostels at which staff could stay while they sought more permanent housing. Despite such efforts it didn't always work out well; as on the morning after an arms theft from Arborfield Barracks, when we lost a number of Irish drivers from the Watford area who we surmised had been involved.

And then there was the 1958 bus strike, when the whole of London Transport's bus operations were closed down for seven weeks. By then the Divisional office had moved to St Albans into that most attractive building which used to face on to the bus terminus (all gone now). Surely my daily cycle ride between Hemel and the office was healthy, though I confess that I gave it up quickly after operations resumed. During the strike there was little to do in the office, but we had to attend for obvious reasons. One day the garage engineer complained about pigeons roosting on the amassed bus roofs inside the garage. One operating official, who was an excellent shot, arranged a shooting party whereby we climbed up the advert fixers' scaffolding and fired off the first round. This certainly disturbed the pigeons sufficiently to prevent any effective second round.

After services were resumed, a difficult period of retrenchment followed, with operations being curtailed, albeit selectively, by about 10%. Despite the obvious pressures, one cannot help feeling that that rapid response stifled any real recovery in passenger use of the buses and contributed to the continuous decline in patronage of the sixties. As it happened, in the summer of 1959 I was suddenly told by my boss to go home and don my smartest suit for an interview later that day at 55 Broadway, as I had been nominated to fill a vacancy for a personal assistant in Board Member Mr Harbour's office. As I have said earlier, such posts were deemed to be outside the standard selection system. I duly attended and was lucky enough to be accepted, an impromptu promotion which in time opened up quite different career prospects. That, however, is another story, though a fitting one on which to end these Country Bus reminiscences.

Green and Red in Redhill

Running bus fleets both in red and green, London Transport sometimes found itself short of vehicles of the appropriate colour. Such a situation has occurred at Reigate garage which these three photos, taken in neighbouring Redhill, illustrate. An elegantly designed London Transport enquiry office can be seen behind green RLH 37. *Alan B Cross collection*

Chicken Runs and Summer Houses

Alan B Cross

Right By the mid-1950s all of the pre-war fleet had been disposed of, but very many vehicles continued to give good service for their new owners, mainly as PSV and contractor's staff transport, but the days of buying them for use as homes and summer houses was over. The caravan sites were being cleared away and declared unfit for habitation, the buses having themselves rotted, being mainly timber framed and beginning to go rotten before their new owners had taken up residence. Vass of Ampthill, Beds, acquired a number of 9T9s and CRs. CR 8, illustrated opposite on a farm near Ampthill, was one of them. In the early post-war years, when there was still much hardship, the only hope some had for a home was to buy an old bus and convert it into somewhere to live. Occasionally one came across a field with little groups of buses all in use as static homes.
Alan B Cross collection/ABC

Sixty years ago, local authority and national planning regulations were far more relaxed compared with today. That which could be "got away with" then would be refused point blank today. Just imagine the furore now if a farmer was to buy a redundant Leyland National, dump it in a field minus wheels and engine in full public view and use it as a chicken run, allowing it succumb to the natural decay of nature with moss-covered broken windows and rusting panels. In the 1950s and earlier, bus enthusiasts would be constantly on the lookout for a bus body behind a hedge, or in a distant field or in a small breaker's yard, many of which were to be found tucked away. Rather like bird watchers who can spot a tiny speck in the sky, bus spotters could pick out a bus body miles away, almost subconsciously, even if it was only part of a roof

By the outbreak of war in 1939 London Transport had largely completed the modernisation and standardisation of some 50% of the fleet and was about to embark on replacing the whole of the LT and ST double deck fleet, which was just about time-expired. The new RT type was ready to go into production but hardly had this commenced than it had to be halted due to the war. In fact 150 of the mistakenly called 'pre-war' RTs were completed and entered service during the first years of the war. The bonus for bus enthusiasts was the doubling of the life of many of these time-expired vehicles. A trickle started to be withdrawn towards the end of 1947, these being vehicles beyond economic overhaul. Numbers swelled in 1948, by the end of which an outside contractor, Cox and Danks, was scrapping bodies on behalf of London Transport, the chassis being returned to Chiswick for spares.

A new firm took over in May 1949, R. L. Daniels, of Rainham, Essex. They were authorised to scrap complete vehicles and additionally allowed to sell on complete vehicles on the condition they would be used other than for PSV work. The most popular sales were single deckers and they were soon to be seen as caravans, summer houses and showmen's vehicles, mainly in and around the home counties. Double deckers went mainly to showmen. Sales by Daniels continued spasmodically into 1951 when their contract ceased. A little later in the '50s the embargo on PSV use was lifted and W. North of Leeds in particular bought up hundreds of London vehicles, many of which saw further service as PSVs and contractors vehicles whilst many others went for export.

The 1/7T7/1 T type was a popular choice because they had sliding front doors and instant security, whereas owners of 'Scooters' and double deckers had to make their own entrance doors before their homes were secure. T 207 became a mobile shop in the Romford area, the body of T 249 was seen on a low loader lorry probably destined to be a caravan, T 252 was on a farm in South Petherton, Devon. T 273 (Fernlea Road, Balham), T 277 (Chevening Halt), T 290 (Corringham), T 297 (Luton, near Chatham) were all caravan homes. T 301 was a mobile booking office for Highway Coaches, in St Albans. On a site in Oldchurch Street, Romford on 20th April 1950 could be seen LT 1169 and ST 1129 in use as homes. The latter provided two storey accommodation and a lot more living space, and still displayed the adverts which it carried in service. Not too far away was another home, LT 1147, in Farington Avenue, Harold Hill, repainted white with a black roof. LT 1059 (a summer house) and 1076 (caravan/home) actually survived long enough to be saved for preservation.

TAILPIECE

Kings Cross coach station was the terminus for a number of old-established medium distance services operated into London by East Anglian independent operators which ran as stage carriages on their outer ends but with very limited stops within the London area. A sunny day finds Premier Travel's Daimler CVD6 No. 73 there before heading back to Haverhill on route 38. This was one of three identical coach seated vehicles purchased in 1950 with bodies by Wilks & Meade, a Wallace Arnold subsidiary. All three carried names; this one was 'County of West Suffolk'. In the background two vehicles of Jennings Coaches from the village of Ashen, near Haverhill, are preparing to load up. This was Jennings's only daily service but they also ran a number of local market day trips to towns on the Essex/Suffolk border such as Halstead, Braintree and Sudbury. These two Leyland/MCW Olympics were the pride of the fleet and replaced a couple of venerable Leyland Cubs on the London run in 1951. *Prince Marshall/KB*